Manifestation of the Tathāgata

Buddhahood According to the *Avataṃsaka Sūtra*

Manifestation of the Tathāgata

Buddhahood According to the *Avataṃsaka Sūtra*

如來性起

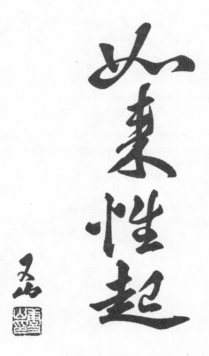

Introduced and Translated by

Cheng Chien Bhikshu

WISDOM PUBLICATIONS
BOSTON

ISBN 0-86171-054-1

WISDOM PUBLICATIONS
361 NEWBURY STREET
BOSTON, MASSACHUSETTS 02115

Library of Congress Cataloging-in-Publication Data

Chien, Cheng, 1964-
Manifestation of the Tathāgata : buddhahood according to the Avataṃsaka Sūtra / introduced and translated by Cheng Chien Bhikshu.
p. cm.
Includes bibliographical references.
ISBN 0-86171-054-1 (pbk. : alk. paper) :
1. Gautama Buddha. 2. Tripiṭaka. Sūtrapiṭaka. Buddhāvataṃsakamahāvaipulyasūtra—Criticism, interpretation, etc. I. Tripiṭaka. Sūtrapiṭaka. Buddhāvataṃsakamahāvaipulyasūtra. English. Selection. 1993. II. Title.
BQ882.C45 1993
294.3'823—dc20 93-24080
CIP

96 97 95 94
10 9 8 7 6 5 4 3 2

Cover Calligraphy by You Shan Tang
Diacritical Garamond created by Pierre Robillard ©1993
Typeset by Andrea Thompson & Andrew Fearnside
Designed by Lisa J. Sawlit

Printed in The United States of America

The Bodhisattvas, seeing the Buddhas, the World-Honored Ones, the dignity of their appearance, fully endowed with all physical marks, whom people rejoice to see, difficult to meet, possessed of great awesome power; or seeing their absolute freedom to appear everywhere, or hearing their prophecies, or harkening their instructions and injunctions, or seeing sentient beings experience all manner of intense suffering, or hearing the vast Buddhadharma of the Tathāgatas, develop bodhicitta *and seek all-encompassing wisdom.*

"Ten Abodes" chapter, *Avataṃsaka Sūtra*

Contents

Foreword

The Indian Mahāyāna sūtras can be divided, according to the chronology of their emergence, into three main groups: early, middle, and late. The two most influential works, the *Prajñāpāramitā Sūtra* and the *Avataṃsaka Sūtra,* belong to the early group, although the *Avataṃsaka Sūtra* and its related texts are thought to have appeared somewhat later than the *Prajñāpāramitā Sūtra.*

The *Prajñāpāramitā* texts teach the supreme meaning of emptiness. The *Avataṃsaka*, however, using this understanding of emptiness as a foundation, establishes the concept of the "miraculous existence of immaculate, limitless worlds." Although the text of the *Avataṃsaka* is vast and complex, it has one dominant theme consistently running through it—a characteristic that may indicate that it is not a collection of shorter sūtras.

From the beginning of Buddhism up to the appearance of the *Avataṃsaka Sūtra*, there was a shift in emphasis from a karmically driven causally originated human existence to a view of the world that is causally originated from Pure Mind. Thus it is said in the *Avataṃsaka* that "everything in the Triple Realm is due to Mind" and "the twelve links of conditioned origination are all dependent on the One Mind."

While the *Prajnāpāramitā* posits the deluded mind as the cause of the twelve-linked chain of conditioned origination, the *Avataṃsaka* speaks about the "Triple Realm" originating from Mind, that is, from Pure Mind. This is the distinctive characteristic of the sūtra. What is the miraculous existence of the immaculate, limitless Pure Mind? The *Avataṃsaka* identifies the entire *dharmadhātu* (universe) as the manifestation of Vairocana—the immaculate, *dharmakāya* Buddha. That precisely is the conditioned origination of the miraculous existence from the Pure Mind.

The *Avataṃsaka Sūtra* circulated throughout India and China in the years A.D. 150–250. The Chinese translations of this sūtra vary in complexity. There exist both simplified and elaborate versions. In addition to the best known versions in eighty, forty, and sixty volumes, there are also forty-three sūtras which, though different, are founded on the same system of thought as the *Avataṃsaka.* Also, the number of volumes varies, some consisting of only one volume, while others consisting of up to ten volumes. For example, there is a translation by the monk Dharmarakṣa (ca. 266–308) of the Western Chin Dynasty entitled *The Appearance of the Tathāgata Sūtra (Ju-lai hsing-hsien ching)* in four volumes. This text is another version of chapter 26 of the eighty-volume *Avataṃsaka*, the "Manifestation of the Tathāgata," under a different title.

Venerable Cheng Chien is accomplished both as a linguist and as an expert in the foundations of the theory of Buddhism. During the past two years he has paid brief visits to both our Institute of Chung-Hwa Culture in New York City and the Dharma Drum Mountain near Taipei. Through these encounters I learned that he was engaged in researching the *Avataṃsaka* and translating the "Manifestation of the Tathāgata" chapter. Recently he presented me with the completed manuscript.

In addition to translating this text, Ven. Cheng Chien has utilized the works of the ancient Chinese Hua-yen scholars, among them Tsung-mi and Li-T'ung Hsuan, in order to help facilitate the reader's comprehension of the material. Most important, however, Ven. Cheng Chien lucidly introduces the reader to the meaning of Buddhahood, as well as explains the origin, transmission, and special features of the *Avataṃsaka*

Sūtra. He also presents us with his understanding of the stature of the "Manifestation of the Tathāgata" chapter in the context of the entire sūtra, as well as its relation to other scholastic texts.

The present volume is an excellent work. It is an honor for me to write this foreword to Ven. Cheng Chien's *Manifestation of the Tathāgata.*

VEN. SHENG-YEN, LITT. D.

Preface

The idea for undertaking the work on the present volume came as a response to a perceived need to provide authentic and authoritative English language texts about Buddhahood. The Buddha and the reality which he symbolizes are the focal point of Buddhism and the source of ultimate refuge for all Buddhists, embodying all their aspiration. The choice of the "Manifestation of the Tathāgata" chapter from the *Avataṃsaka Sūtra* for this purpose was a natural one for two reasons. First, the "Manifestation of the Tathāgata" chapter is one of the most important sections of the *Avataṃsaka Sūtra.* Long esteemed by the Buddhist followers in the Far East, this chapter (or *sūtra*) is among the most comprehensive and authoritative texts on the nature of Buddhahood from the perspective of the One Vehicle teaching. The second reason is a personal one. This text is one of my favorite chapters of the *Avataṃsaka Sūtra*; a *sūtra* that over time has proven to be the most valuable source of inspiration and guidance in my religious cultivation, and that I believe can play a major role in the growth of Buddhism in the West. It is my hope that this translation, with all its imperfections, will help to focus more attention on this important text.

The present translation was done from the Śikṣānanda's eighty-*chüan* Chinese translation. In this translation I have tried to keep to the original as closely as possible. In certain instances when a particular passage could have been read in different ways, I have followed the reading of Ch'eng-kuan Ta-shih (738–839) as found in his standard commentary on the sūtra. The Chinese editions of the text of the "Manifestation of the Tathāgata" chapter and Ch'eng-kuan's commentary used for the present volume are those from Tao-p'ei, ed., *Hua-yen ching shu lun tsuan-yao (Compilation of the Explication and the Comments on the Avataṃsaka Sūtra).* The Taishō references of Ch'eng-kuan's commentary are for reference only.

A previous translation of the Manifestation of the Tathāgata" chapter under the title "Manifestation of the Buddha" appeared in Thomas Cleary, *The Flower Ornament Scripture*, vol. 2 (Boston and London: Shambhala, 1986), pp. 282–333. I often consulted this translation during the preparation of the present translation, and wish to acknowledge my indebtedness to it. Considering its scope, Dr. Cleary's work is truly commendable; however, there are certain aspects of his translation that allow for improvement. Among them are his rather free style, and his tendency to translate every technical term into English, even when the original Sanskrit is more familiar than his own renditions.

In addition, not only does the sheer volume of the entire scripture put off many readers, but its intricacy, comprehensiveness, and profuse use of symbolism and imagery can prove insurmountable obstacles for even those brave enough to try to tackle its mysteries. It seems to me that a useful approach might be to present the important chapters of the *Avataṃsaka*—which by themselves are independent sūtras—as individual volumes with the appropriate introductory material and annotation to assist the present-day reader. This approach should, of course, supplement the study of the whole sūtra, not replace it. I hope this volume will be followed by others that in a similar way will present the other principal chapters of the *Avataṃsaka.*

The transliterations from the Chinese in this volume are in the Wade-Giles system. The definitions of Buddhist terms usually follow those given in William Edward Soothill and Lewis Hodous, *A Dictionary of Chinese Buddhist Terms* (Kao-hsiung,

Taiwan: Fo-kuang ch'u-pan she, 1962) and/or Ting Fu-pao, *Fo-hsüeh ta ts'u-tien,* in two volumes (Taipei: Hua-tsang fo-chiao t'u-shu kuan, 1988) The following abbreviations have been used throughout this volume:

T *Taishō shinshū daizōkyō,* edited by Takakusu Junjirō and Watanabe Kaigyoku.

HTC *Hsü tsang ching,* a Taiwanese reprint of Dainippon zokuzōkyō.

HYCS *Hua-yen ching shu,* by Ch'eng-kuan.

Acknowledgments

I wish to express my gratitude to the following individuals who contributed to the preparation of this volume: Ko Chiren for comparing most of the translation with the original Chinese text; Stuart Lachs and Cynthia Durgan for reading parts of the manuscript, especially the Introduction, and offering useful suggestions for possible improvements; and Elizabeth Goreham and Jack Matson for expressing interest in my work and providing practical help toward the production of the manuscript. My deep appreciation goes to Nick Ribush, Timothy McNeill, and the staff of Wisdom Publications for their interest in my work and their expertise in the production of this volume. Their dedication to bringing the Dharma to the West serves as a fine example of actively putting the teaching into practice. My special thanks are due to Ven. Sheng Yen for honoring me by assenting to write the Foreword. I also wish to acknowledge the support from Jerry Pan, as well as from Liu Te-wen and the numerous faithful associated with the Texas Buddhist Association, without whose generosity it might have been impossible to bring out this volume in its present form. To them, and to all others who are dedicated to the Buddha's Path of wisdom and compassion, this volume is dedicated.

Part One

Introduction

The Conception of Buddhahood

From the very beginnings of Buddhism the first step toward becoming a Buddhist follower has consisted in taking the three refuges—the refuges in the Buddha, the Dharma, and the Saṅgha. The three refuges embody the highest ideals of Buddhism, and provide the ultimate source of inspiration and guidance for the Buddhist follower. Often the three refuges are viewed as three aspects of one reality. This interrelatedness of the three refuges is indicated by the well-known saying of the Buddha about his relationship with the Dharma, as recorded in the Pāli canon: "He who sees the Dhamma (Dharma) sees me; he who sees me sees the Dhamma. For it is when he sees the Dhamma that he sees me; and it is when he sees me that he sees the Dhamma."[1] With this kind of understanding, sometimes for the sake of better focus the three refuges are condensed into one, which is referred to as the "ultimate refuge." This is the "one essence" which manifests as three.[2]

Most often the choice for representing the ultimate refuge falls on the Buddha. That is so in part because for most people the Buddha is the easiest of the three refuges to relate to, and is the most suitable object for the development of faith, which plays an essential role in the cultivation of the Path (*mārga*). So it is natural that we speak of Buddhism (the religion or teaching of the Buddha or about the Buddha), and of Buddhists (the followers of the Buddha). One may, then, conclude that for anyone seriously interested in Buddhism, be it as a philosophical system and a phenomenon in religious history, or in a more personal way as a vehicle of spiritual liberation, the understanding of the concept of Buddhahood should be of paramount importance.

What is meant by the Buddha? What is Buddhahood? Can we achieve it? And if so, by what means can it be achieved? These are some of the questions that naturally arise in the course of thoughtful consideration of the teaching of the Buddha.

Some Meanings of the Term "Buddhahood"

As even a cursory reading of works on the subject of Buddhism soon reveals, words such as Buddha and Buddhahood are often used in various senses. Normally the term "Buddhahood" is used in a broader conceptual context than the term "Buddha" and has more pronounced impersonal connotations, though the two are often interchangeable. When encountering the term "Buddha" what first comes to mind is the monk who after attaining enlightenment "turned the wheel of the Dharma, which is sublime in the beginning, sublime in the middle, and sublime in the end." This is the Buddha who would put on his robe and go for alms, instruct his disciples, and go to rest at night. The great teacher who initiated one of the great world religions, established the Order that preserved his teaching over the centuries (albeit in a number of different formulations), became old and passed away. Śākyamuni Buddha, or Gotama the Buddha, is the enlightened being to whom Buddhists are eternally indebted for the teaching that leads to the purification of mind and enables one to experience that perfect freedom which cannot be shaken by anything, a teaching that is always accessible to those who are sincere and have faith.

Besides the historical Buddha the scriptures also speak of numerous other Buddhas, such as Kāśyapa Buddha and Akṣobhya Buddha. All these Buddhas are said to be identical in their realization and the virtue they manifest, thus forming a lineage of Buddhas of which Śākyamuni is only the last one to appear in this world.

But often we come to another image of the Buddha: a Buddha whose body pervades the universe, in whose single pore numberless worlds are revealed, who is eternally expounding the Dharma. And even further, sometimes the Buddha is spoken of as emptiness, suchness, the inconceivable reality, the absolute. This is the Buddha whose "body is unborn" and whose "essential nature is quiescent and without any characteristics."[3] Here the term is obviously used as an appellation of ultimate reality, rather than of a person.

These different senses in which the term "Buddha" is used have often led to some confusion. A number of disputes and misunderstandings within the Buddhist community from the earliest times have revolved around the status of the Buddha and the nature of Buddhahood. For example, those who are used to the term as commonly employed in the sūtras of the Pāli canon are often baffled when they encounter in the Mahāyāna scriptures the depiction of the Buddha as (what appears to be) a godlike transcendent being. Hence there are accusations about "corrupting influences" from Hinduism, supposedly contrary to the spirit of "original Buddhism." Or when people take literally or out of context some of the statements and symbolism used for the sake of illustration in the Mahāyāna scriptures they are liable to commit gross category mistakes or conceive of all kinds of superstitions. This is usually accompanied by the loss of sight of the ordinariness of the Buddha as a person, and often leads to an attitude that precludes any attempt toward genuine personal transformation.

First of all, terms such as "Buddha" and "Buddhahood" are just that—mere words that assume the meanings we give to them. Many of the arguments in Buddhism are due to overlooking this simple fact. Often proponents of different doctrines simply ignore the definitions of the cardinal concepts and the contexts in which they are used by their self-assigned opponents.

Imputing their own understanding of the concepts and doctrines under discussion, they try to prove their fallacy.[4]

When trying to understand a concept such as "Buddhahood," it is important to distinguish between the different senses in which the term is used. This is not always an easy task, since often even within a short passage the same term can be used with a variety of connotations with still subtler nuances. In some scriptures, such as the *Avataṃsaka Sūtra*, this technique is often used in order to help the reader to develop an intuitive understanding of the different shades of meaning and integrate them in a holistic, all-inclusive awareness that is able to perceive things as they truly are.

A useful device for distinguishing the different levels of meaning of Buddhahood is the doctrine of the three bodies of the Buddha. The three bodies are (1) *dharmakāya*, the essential body of the Buddha, which corresponds to the ultimate reality, (2) *sambhogakāya*, the body of reward, which in its glorified form is revealed to the Bodhisattvas, and (3) *nirmāṇakāya*, the transformation body, which is the physical body of the Buddha as manifest in the human realm. When using this classical Mahāyāna doctrine, however, it is useful to bear in mind that the three bodies lack self-nature and are just three aspects of one ineffable reality, and each body implies the other two. Sometimes only two bodies are spoken of; it is also possible to speak of ten bodies, or some other number, depending on the number of perspectives from which Buddhahood is observed.

The three bodies and their mutual interrelatedness is well illustrated in the last chapter of the *Avataṃsaka Sūtra*, the "Entering the *Dharmadhātu*" chapter. Toward the end of the chapter, after Sudhana, the main hero of the scripture, has visited all other teachers in his quest for enlightenment, he comes to Maitreya, the future Buddha, to inquire about the Bodhisattvas' practice. Having witnessed the miraculous display in the Tower of the Store of Vairocana's Adornments, Sudhana asks Maitreya where he comes from. In response Maitreya describes the place of his origin in three different ways. While Maitreya speaks about the place of coming of the Bodhisattvas, the description equally applies to Buddhahood, as the context and the explanation given below demonstrate. First he says:

> All Bodhisattvas have no coming and going—thus do they come. They come from where there is no activity or abiding. They come from where there is no abode or attachment, no passing away or birth, no stability or change, no movement or arising, no desire or attachment, no action or result, no creation or destruction, no annihilation or permanence.[5]

Maitreya continues his explanation by shifting the focus of his exposition to another level of meaning. The Bodhisattvas also come—that is, are produced—from great compassion, great kindness, pure discipline, great vows, non-attachment, wisdom, skillful methods, etc. Then Maitreya ends his answer by shifting his perspective once more, and tells Sudhana that he comes from a village called Kuti in his native country Malayadesa.

According to the comments on this passage given by Ch'eng-kuan (738–839),[6] the reputed fourth patriarch of the Hua-yen tradition, in his reply Maitreya explains "the place from where all Bodhisattvas come" (i.e., Buddhahood) from three perspectives, which are correlated to the three bodies of the Buddha. First is the perspective of the "essence" (*t'i*), which is encompassed in the first part of Maitreya's reply. In terms of the three bodies of the Buddha it corresponds to the *dharmakāya*. This is the essential nature, or the ultimate reality, in which coming and going lose their identity. Because the *dharmakāya* is beyond the sphere of thought and perception, the text presents a series of negations to point to the realm that is beyond conceptual imagination.

The second perspective is that of the characteristics (*hsiang*); it is encompassed in the second part of Maitreya's reply and corresponds to the *sambhogakāya*, which is born from the myriad practices of the Bodhisattvas. The third perspective is that of the function (*yung*) of Buddhahood; it is its active aspect, which is represented by the *nirmāṇakāya*, the physical body that appears in the world in response to conditions in order to benefit sentient beings.[7] The *nirmāṇakāya* is alluded to in the last part of Maitreya's reply where he claims Malayadesa (presumably a locality in India) as his native place.

When speaking in terms of principle (*li*) and phenomena (*shih*),[8] the *dharmakāya* corresponds to the principle, the *nirmāṇakāya* to phenomena, while the *sambhogakāya* is the meeting ground of both.[9] This explication has direct implications for our understanding of the ways the different aspects of Buddhahood are mutually related.

The limitations of the view that attaches to the Buddha as a person, while a perfectly understandable human tendency with a useful role in the course of religious cultivation, are often pointed out in the sūtras. For example, there are the following verses in the *Avataṃsaka Sūtra*:

> If someone would for a hundred thousand kalpas
> Constantly look at the Tathāgata
> Without relying on ultimate reality,
> But [only] seeing the world's savior,
>
> That person is attaching to forms,
> And enlarging the net of ignorance and illusion;
> Tied up to the prison of birth and death,
> Deluded, he does not see the Buddha.[10]

The purpose of the teaching of the Buddha is not to set up some special being as an object of worship and bestower of liberation, but to point to the eternal reality that can be realized by anyone. That is the reason why in the first few centuries of Buddhist history the main object of worship for the Buddha's followers was the *stūpa*, which represents the Buddha as the formless reality realized by him. As someone who has perfectly comprehended the ultimate reality—or rather has realized his identity with it—and is able to direct others to it, the Buddha symbolizes that reality. Thus his importance lies primarily in what he signifies and indicates to others, rather than what he was as a person.

But disregarding the Buddha as a person and trying to take the teaching completely out of its historical context is also an attitude based on limited understanding. After all, if it were not for the Buddha there would not have been any knowledge about the Buddhadharma in the world. As the *Avataṃsaka Sūtra* states:

> Like a jewel in darkness
> Which cannot be seen without a lamp,
> If there is no one to explain the Buddhadharma,
> Even among the wise no one can realize it.[11]

As demonstrated by the Hua-yen teaching of the interpenetration and mutual identity of the principle and phenomena (about which more will be said below), a more correct outlook would be one that would simultaneously include the different aspects of Buddhahood in an all-inclusive perspective in which they harmoniously interrelate in perfect freedom and non-obstruction. Or, from the viewpoint of practice,

> If someone wishes to know the realm of the Buddha,
> He should purify his mind [so that it becomes] like space;
> Forsaking false thoughts and attachments,
> Having the mind unobstructed amidst all objects.[12]

Significance for Religious Cultivation

Keeping in mind the different conceptions of Buddhahood, we can develop a better appreciation of its centrality in Buddhism as both the source of the Path and its various formulations, as well as the ultimate goal of the Path. Buddhahood is the central point of Buddhism from which flow the numerous elements that constitute that tradition, and to which they constantly refer and ultimately return.

Buddhahood is the source of the Path within both a historical and conceptual context. From a historical perspective, the various doctrines that elaborate on the form and substance of the Path all have their roots—or at least claim to have—in the Buddha's experience of perfect enlightenment. On a different level, Buddhahood is the source of the Path inasmuch as it is the "seed" present in sentient beings that causes them to aspire toward enlightenment. This seed, according to a certain line of thought, is the pure luminous mind, which is only adventitiously covered with defilements. Simultaneously, Buddhahood is the primordial ground upon which one's practice takes place, which when properly done leads to reversion to the original state of perfect freedom, bliss, and clarity—the state of Buddhahood.

In relation to the realm of practice, Buddhahood can be perceived as the starting point of ones cultivation, the source of guidance during its course, and its final result. It is the starting point because the Buddha and his enlightenment, as the most exalted source of inspiration, serve as the focal object of faith. Faith is an essential quality and prerequisite for any kind of practice, which is why it is regarded as the "source of the Path." As it is stated in the *Avataṃsaka Sūtra*:

> Faith is the source of the Path and Mother of virtue;
> Providing nourishment to all wholesome dharmas,
> Obliterating the web of doubts and leading away from the stream of desire,
> It shows the supreme path to Nirvāṇa.[13]

During the course of practice Buddhahood also serves as a

source of direction and guidance for one's cultivation. The active aspect of Buddhahood manifests as the "myriad virtues and practices," the development of which constitutes the Path. Those qualities that are fully developed by the Buddha, and that are constantly manifested in his activity—wisdom, kindness, compassion, etc.—are also the very qualities that have to be developed by the aspiring practitioner. In addition, Buddhahood also provides a framework of standards for evaluating Buddhist teachers, teachings, and spiritual attainments. Clear conceptual understanding of what the Buddha and his teaching stand for (and what they never stand for) can be of enormous use in delineating the actual form and substance of one's involvement with Buddhism. Familiarity with the basic concepts of Buddhism is essential for installing a mature, responsible, and realistic attitude toward the Path. In the case of Buddhahood, that familiarity also helps one to develop a more humble attitude, which in turn prevents one from grasping limited subjective states as constituting any attainment.

Buddhahood is also, ideally, the ultimate goal of Buddhist practice. That is to say, the main purpose of Buddhist doctrines is to elaborate a course of religious practice that results in the realization of the perfect freedom the Buddha experienced under the *bodhi* tree.

In light of its centrality to Buddhist theory and practice, in this volume we present a few perspectives on the meaning, characteristics, and significance of Buddhahood. While the text chosen for that purpose is one that has been regarded over the centuries with the greatest esteem by the Buddhists in East Asia, it should be obvious that it is presented from a particular perspective and can only point to the sublime wonder of Buddhahood in a way that is only partially adequate. As the scriptures repeatedly emphasize, Buddhahood is beyond the sphere of thought and language. In order to *fully* understand Buddhahood, one has to become a Buddha. Because of this, it is often presumed that since the ultimate depth of Buddhahood is not something that can be apprehended on a conceptual level, any attempt toward its conceptual understanding is futile. Yet for almost everyone the highest form of knowing is that which takes place on the conceptual plane, and when we encounter any concept such as Buddhahood, we typically impute some meaning to it. While no explanation, however complete and profound, can ever capture the mystery of Buddhahood (or any similar concept), some forms of understanding are more correct than others. And some are completely wrong. Right and wrong, of course, not in an absolute sense, but in a sense of being or not being conducive to liberation. The kind of basic belief system and conceptual understanding one has—even if one adheres to the fiction of having none—will determine the nature of one's practice and the issuing result—or the lack of it.

Understanding the basic teachings of Buddhism is essential, but that is only one factor in the quest for final liberation. Understanding has to be accompanied with practice and supported by faith. When all of these are fully developed, realization naturally follows.

The *Avataṃsaka Sūtra*

Origins and Transmission

An ancient Buddhist tradition relates that after the Buddha realized perfect enlightenment under the bodhi tree in the country of Magadha, from his unobstructed transcendental awareness grounded on his immediate vision of reality he expounded the *Avataṃsaka Sūtra* to the vast assembly at the site of enlightenment. The teaching of the sūtra, being a direct expression of the Buddha's realization, discloses the ultimate reality in a "complete and sudden" manner, without any attempt to adjust the exposition to the capacity of the audience. For that reason, when the Buddha expounded the doctrines of the *Avataṃsaka,* the story goes, for the most part the listeners stood "as deaf and dumb," failing to understand the teaching which was beyond their power of comprehension. Therefore, for guiding beings inveterate in ignorance, the Buddha resorted to the soteriological contrivance of formulating his instructions in different ways to meet the various abilities of his listeners. From this arose the so-called teachings of the three vehicles.

In accord with the notion that the *Avataṃsaka Sūtra* epitomizes the consummate expression of the enlightened mind, the Buddha who figures most prominently throughout the text is Vairocana Buddha. Vairocana represents the absolute aspect of universal Buddhahood. The written version of the sūtra available to humanity is said to be just an extract of the infinite sūtra, eternal and absolute, identical with the ultimate reality of the *dharmadhātu.*[14] This eternal version is said to have been taught by Vairocana Buddha in the Lotus Treasury world while he was immersed in the Ocean Seal *samādhi*. Being beyond the realm of words and transcending time and space, this sūtra defies all attempts to place it within a historical, cultural, or social context.

Nonetheless, the text of the *Avataṃsaka* has been a subject of historical analysis. While there is much that remains unclear about its early provenance, the present state of knowledge seems to suggest that the origins of the text as a literary document can be traced back to the beginning of the Christian era. Since many of the chapters of the *Avataṃsaka* exist as independent sūtras, it seems plausible that unknown editors have compiled the various texts into a single volume. The paucity of references to the sūtra in Indian treatises coupled with the appearance of names of sites in Central Asia have led some scholars to even suggest that the texts had been put together outside of India, presumably in the Central Asian area of Khotan.[15] This is further corroborated by the fact that many of the translators of the various sūtras belonging to the *Avataṃsaka* corpus were monks from Central Asia.

However, there is no doubt that different versions of the sūtra existed in India, since there are extant manuscripts of the two most important, as well as longest, chapters of the sūtra preserved in Sanskrit as independent sūtras: the *Daśabhūmika Sūtra* (*Ten Stages Sūtra*) and the *Gaṇḍavyūha Sūtra*. The *Daśabhūmika Sūtra* was—together with its commentary written by Vasubandu, the *Daśabhūmivyākhyāna*, translated into Chinese ca. 508 by Bodhiruci and Ratnamati—a subject of intense study among the learned monks of sixth century China. That was the case especially with those monks who were associated with the Ti-lun school, which was based on its doctrines. The *Gandavyūha Sūtra* corresponds to the longest and most popular chapter of the *Avataṃsaka*. Both of these texts can be traced back to the third century at the latest on evidence of extant Chinese translations. Moreover, the fact that at certain times parts of the sūtra existed as independent sūtras is by no means a clear indication that the whole text did not exist at the same time. It is well known that for a few centuries after the first Chinese translation of the complete text of the *Avataṃsaka* individual chapters were being translated into Chinese as independent sūtras.

The oldest extant text of the *Avataṃsaka* corpus in Chinese translation is the *Fo shuo t'u-sha ching (Tuṣita Sūtra)* in one *chüan*, translated by the Central Asian monk Lokakṣin sometime between 178–189.[16] Other early translations of parts of the sūtra are the *P'u-sa penyeh ching (Bodhisattva's Original Acts Sūtra)* in one *chüan*,[17] translated between 222–228 by Chih-ch'ien, a monk from Yueh-chih who came to Lo-yang toward the end of the Later Han Dynasty (25–220); and the *Fo shuo Lo-mo-ch'ieh ching* in three *chüan*,[18] an earlier version of the "Entering the *Dharmadhātu*" chapter, translated between 220–264 by An Fa-hsien, which is unfortunately lost.

There are a few theories about the original title of the *Avataṃsaka*.[19] The most widely accepted reconstruction of the original Sanskrit title is *Buddhāvataṃsaka-nāmamahāvaipulya Sūtra*. The first complete translation of the *Avataṃsaka Sūtra* into Chinese was done by Buddhabhadra (359–429)[20] between 418–421. This translation is in sixty *chüan* and has thirty-four chapters; its full title in Chinese is *Ta-fang-kuang fo hua-yen ching*.[21] A native of Northern India, Buddhabhadra was a disciple of Buddhasena. He was a monk of the Sarvāstivāda school which was flourishing in Kashmir, where he spent his formative monastic years. Besides being a scholar and translator, Buddhabhadra was also renowned as a specialist in meditation. A new translation of the sūtra under the same title was completed under the patronage of Empress Wu (r. 685–705) during the 695–704 period by the Khotanese monk Śikṣānanda (652–710).[22] This translation is in eighty *chüan*, and has thirty-nine chapters.[23] The two translations are quite similar, the second being perhaps more literal and somewhat longer because it contains new material not found in the older version.

A third forty-*chüan* translation was done between 795–798 by Prajñā,[24] another monk from Northern India who specialized in Sarvāstivāda Buddhism.[25] This version consists only of the final chapter of the other two versions and never gained the popularity enjoyed by the other two. Besides the Chinese translations of the *Avataṃsaka*, there exists a Tibetan translation. Translated around 878–901 by the Indian monks Jinamitra and Surendrabodhi with the help of Ye-śes-sde, this translation is longer than any of the Chinese translations.[26]

Distinctive Features

Held in highest esteem by the followers of the native Buddhist traditions of East Asia, the text of the *Avataṃsaka* is of truly encyclopedic proportions, being one of the longest in the *tripiṭaka*. All of the important tenets of Mahāyāna Buddhism can be found in the sūtra, making it one of the most comprehensive compendiums of the Buddhist teaching. The doctrines of the philosophical systems of Indian Buddhism, which were formulated during the first few centuries of the present era, are set in it side by side in a concurrent way, each complementing and shedding more light on the others, thus revealing the Bodhisattva Path in its full depth, glory, and perfection. The principal systems are the Mādhyamika with its apophatic approach based on the teaching of *śūnyatā*, which reveals the absence of inherent self-nature in all phenomena and their dependent origination; the more positive approach of Yogācāra, with its overriding concern of the role of consciousness in the establishment of phenomenal reality, as well as with its transformation which culminates in the attainment of enlightenment; and the Tathāgatagarbha doctrine of the intrinsically pure mind. This, of course, does not imply that the sūtra is concerned with the presentation of any of these philosophical systems, or that it is meant to fulfill the same purpose as those treatises that attempt to present the doctrines of a particular Buddhist school. On the contrary, while subsuming all doctrines, the *Avataṃsaka* simultaneously transcends them all and directly discloses the primordial ground from where all doctrines spring, and to which they finally return.

An often quoted feature of the sūtra's exposition of the myriad aspects of the Path is that all of them are presented in the light of the integrative perspective of the one true *dharmadhātu*, of which the mutual non-obstruction and interpenetration among phenomena are salient features stated in a way unique to the *Avataṃsaka*. This theme was extensively elaborated by the Huayen masters, and is perhaps more representative of their thought than of the text of the sūtra, though ample evidence for these principles is not lacking in the sūtra itself.

While the *Avataṃsaka* is often understood as a description of the Buddha's enlightenment or a mine of illustrations for the doctrines mentioned above (as well as other doctrines not alluded to), the sūtra can best be appreciated as a practical guide for the Bodhisattva's way of practice. Most of the *Avataṃsaka* is primarily concerned with presenting a detailed explanation of the whole career of a Bodhisattva, from the awakening of *bodhicitta* to the accomplishment of perfect Buddhahood. The Bodhisattva Path is presented in the *Avataṃsaka* in four sets of ten stages, culminating with the two levels of enlightenment. The Bodhisattva Path starts with the awakening of *bodhicitta*, the infinite mind of great compassion set on perfect enlightenment (its noumenal aspect) and salvation of all sentient beings (its phenomenal aspect), which occurs on the first of the ten abodes (*daśa-vihāra*). Then follow the ten practices (*daśa-caryā*), the ten dedications (*daśa-pariṇāmanā*), and the ten stages (*daśa-bhūmi*).

To these four sets of ten articles the commentators have added the ten faiths (*daśa-śraddhā*), which precede the ten abodes and thus form the initial stages of the Path. The Bodhisattva's practice culminates in the attainment of the two levels of equal and sublime enlightenment. When the noumenal realm of fundamental perfection and the phenomenal realm of selfless activity are fully developed in a perfectly balanced way, then wisdom and compassion reach their full potential and, transcending bounds and measures, the Bodhisattva reaches the ultimate stage of Buddhahood.

Influence on Chinese Buddhism

Together with the *Lotus Sūtra*, the *Avataṃsaka Sūtra* has over the centuries occupied the place of highest prominence among the Buddhist scriptures in China and the rest of East Asia. Its profound teaching has inspired and edified countless students of the Buddhadharma, and its rich imagery and symbolism have given stimulus to many admirable artistic enterprises. The *Avataṃsaka* exerted great influence on the development of the native Chinese Buddhist traditions. That influence is most readily observable in the case of the Hua-yen school, as the name of the school suggests, Hua-yen being the Chinese translation of *Avataṃsaka.* Points of influence can also to varying degrees be found in the teachings of all new traditions that were formed during the Sui-T'ang period.

The *Avataṃsaka* provided the scriptural basis for the doctrines of the great Hua-yen school. This school's stupendous system was formulated by Chih-yen and Fa-tsang, who later came to be regarded as the second and third patriarchs of the school respectively. The Hua-yen system was further refined by its reputed fourth patriarch Ch'eng-kuan. In many ways this school is considered the highest point of doctrinal development in East Asian Buddhism, whose vision continues to provide an immensely satisfying view of reality. It is a view of great profundity, beauty, and meaningfulness, which can serve as a unifying factor for bringing the many fragmented facets of human experience and activity into focus. The texts of the Hua-yen school contain much invaluable material for understanding the *Avataṃsaka.* They can also serve as excellent manuals for contemplation, as well as provide inspiring and meaningful theory for spiritual practice. Much of the influence the *Avataṃsaka* has exerted on East Asian Buddhism has been through the teaching of the Hua-yen school, which served as catalyst for disseminating the message of the sūtra to the wider audience of East Asian Buddhists.[27]

The *Avataṃsaka* was also much used by the Ch'an school, to which testify the copious motifs and quotations from the sūtra in the records of the Ch'an masters. The teaching of Ma-tsu's (709–788) Hung-chou school—which after the ninth century became the most widespread and vital Buddhist school in China—is closely associated with the *Avataṃsaka.* Presence of Hua-yen themes can also be discerned in the teachings of Matsu's illustrious contemporary Shih-t'ou Hsi-ch'ien (700–790), especially in his famous poem *Ts'an-t'ung ch'i.*[28] The same influence can be found in the five ranks teaching of Tung-shan Liang-chieh (807-869) and Ts'ao-shan Pen-chi (840–901), the reputed founding teachers of the Ts'ao-tung school of Ch'an, and in the sermons of Fa-yen Wen-i (885–958), who is considered to be the founder of the Fa-yen school of Ch'an. The close relationship between Ch'an and the *Avataṃsaka*—or, perhaps more accurately, Hua-yen—is perhaps best exemplified in the person and thought of Tsung-mi, one of the most noted monks of T'ang China. Besides being a Ch'an master, Tsungmi was also recognized as the fifth, and last, patriarch of the Hua-yen tradition.

The *Avataṃsaka*'s influence continued throughout the later

course of Ch'an history, and is especially noticeable in the thought of Chinul (1158–1210), who during the Koryo Dynasty (937–1392) revived the declining fortunes of the Ch'an school in Korea. Chinul was profoundly influenced by Tsung-mi, as can be discerned by the numerous quotations from Tsung-mi's writings in Chinul's works. Another important influence on Chinul was that of Li T'ung-hsüan (635–730), also an important Hua-yen figure. The *Avataṃsaka*'s influence on Ch'an has been such that it has even been suggested that Ch'an is the practical expression of the profound and comprehensive teaching of the *Avataṃsaka*.

From the sixth century on the *Avataṃsaka* also served as an object of veneration for numerous Chinese Buddhists, to which testify numerous stories about miraculous occurrences attributed to the power of the sūtra. The cults based on the worship of the sūtra provided meaningful ways of bringing together great numbers of men and women in devotional acts of penance, recitation of the sūtra, and participation in vegetarian feasts. These communal acts of worship enabled all those who would have otherwise found the abstruse doctrines of the sūtra overly perplexing to deepen their faith, acquire merit, and plant wholesome seeds that, at some later date when the right conditions are present, will blossom in the fruition of unobstructed wisdom.

THE "MANIFESTATION OF THE TATHĀGATA" CHAPTER

Chinese Translations and Commentaries

The oldest extant Chinese translation of the "Manifestation of the Tathāgata" chapter of the Avataṃsaka Sūtra (henceforth abbreviated to the "Manifestation" chapter) is *Ju-lai hsing-hsien ching* (*The Appearance of the Tathāgata Sūtra*) in four *chüan*,[29] translated by the Indo-Scythian monk Dharmarakṣa (Fa-hu, active ca. 266–308).[30] Born in Tun-huang sometime around 230, Dharmarakṣa is considered the greatest translator of the period before the coming of Kumārajīva (344–413). Fluent in both Chinese and Sanskrit, as well as many other Central Asian languages, he translated 159 works, of which 72 have been preserved. Among them is the first translation of the immensely influential *Lotus Sūtra*.[31] During most of his translation and teaching career Dharmarakṣa was active in Ch'ang-an, and he is the person most responsible for its transformation into an important center of Buddhist studies.

The ancient texts also provide information about three other translations of the "Manifestation" chapter done about the same time, all of which are no longer extant. They are: (1) *Ta-fang-kuang ju-lai hsing-ch'i ching* (*Extensive Universal Nature Origination of the Tathāgata Sūtra*) in two *chüan*. Its translator is unknown, and it includes the "Names of the Buddhas" chapter of the complete translation of the *Avataṃsaka* as its preface; (2) *Ju-lai hsing-hsien ching* (*The Appearance of the Tathāgata Sūtra*) in one *chüan*, translated by Po Fa-tsu during the Western Chin

Dynasty (265–313); and (3) *Ta-fang-kuang ju-lai hsing-ch'i wei-mi-tsang ching* (*Extensive Universal Arcane Store of the Nature Origination of the Tathāgata Sūtra*) in two *chüan*, also translated during the Western Chin Dynasty by an unknown translator.

In Buddhabhadra's sixty-*chüan* translation of the *Avataṃsaka* the "Manifestation" chapter is chapter 32. Its title is *Pao-wang ju-lai hsing-ch'i p'in*, or "Nature Origination of Precious King Tathāgata" chapter.[32] Its Sanskrit title has been reconstructed as *Tathāgatotpatti-sambhava-nirdeśa*. It is from the title of this chapter that the appellation of the important Hua-yen concept of nature origination was taken. In Śikṣānanda's translation of the *Avataṃsaka* the "Manifestation" chapter is chapter 37, and its title in Chinese is *Ju-lai ch'u-hsien p'in*.

While no commentary on Dharmarakṣa's translation has been written, commentaries on the "Manifestation" chapter can be found in the standard commentaries on the *Avataṃsaka* which provide chapter by chapter exegesis of the whole text of the sūtra. The oldest two, done on the sixty-*chüan* version, are: (1) Chih-yen's *Hua-yen ching sou-hsüan chi* (*Record of Investigation into the Mysteries of Avataṃsaka Sūtra*) in five *chüan*,[33] written in 628 when Chih-yen was twenty-six years old; and (2) Fa-tsang's *Hua-yen ching t'an-hsüan chi* (*Record of Inquiry into the Mysteries of Avataṃsaka Sūtra*)[34] in twenty *chüan*. Though the second replaced the first, it is in many ways indebted to its predecessor.

Commentaries on Śikṣānanda's translation of the "Manifestation" chapter can be found in: (1) *Hsü hua-yen ching lueh-shu k'an-ting chi (Final Version of the Record of the Continuation of the Brief Explication of the Avataṃsaka)*,[35] in fifteen *chüan*, written by Hui-yüan (673–743), the most renowned among the numerous disciples of Fa-tsang; (2) Ch'eng-kuan's *Hua-yen ching shu* (*Explication of the Avataṃsaka Sūtra*) in sixty *chüan*,[36] which is the most detailed and authoritative commentary on the *Avataṃsaka*; and (3) *Hsin hua-yen ching lun* (*Comments on the New [Translation of the] Avataṃsaka Sūtra*),[37] written by Li T'ung-hsüan toward the end of his life. The last commentary seems to have passed largely unnoticed during the time of its writing and the ensuing few centuries. However, by the time of the Sung Dynasty (960–1279) it gained in approbation, especially among the members of the Ch'an school for whom the simplicity of Li T'ung-hsüan's exegesis as well as his strong emphasis on practical application of the teachings contained in the sūtra had a strong appeal. The two commentaries of Ch'eng-kuan and Li T'ung-hsüan were combined together with the text of the sūtra into a single volume in 1669 by the Ching Dynasty (1644–1912) monk Tao-p'ei under the title *Hua-yen ching shu lun tsuan-yao (Compilation of the Explication and the Comments on the Avataṃsaka Sūtra)*.

Position in the Avataṃsaka Sūtra

In his comment on the meaning of the occurrence of the "Manifestation" chapter in its position within the chapter sequence of the *Avataṃsaka*, Ch'eng-kuan says:

> The previous chapters explained the 'cause' *(hetu, yin)* of the 'fruit' *(phala, kuo)*. This chapter discerns the fruit of the cause. Though the essence is equal, the two features are not effaced—the cause comes first, while the fruit comes later.[38]

The two terms cause and fruit (or result) are used here within the context of the quest and attainment of enlightenment as they are outlined in the *Avataṃsaka*. "Cause" refers to the cultivation of the myriad practices of the Bodhisattva, while "fruit" refers to the realization of the primordial quiescence of Nirvāṇa, i.e., the attainment of Buddhahood. Explaining the meaning of cause and fruit in his *Hua-yen i-sheng shih hsüan men (Ten Recondite Principles of the One Vehicle of the Avataṃsaka)*, Chih-yen says:

> That which is referred to as cause are the expedient means of conditioned cultivation by which the essence is traced to the very source and the stages [of the Path] are consummated, which is [symbolized by] Samantabhadra, while that which is referred to as fruit is the perfect fruition of the absolute quiescence of that essence, [symbolized by] the realm of the ten Buddhas.[39]

Therefore, after the preceding chapters of the *Avataṃsaka* have expounded the practice of Samantabhadra, which is the cultivation of all virtuous qualities that comprise the Bodhisattva Path, the "Manifestation" chapter presents the consummation of the sūtra, revealing the final result of the Bodhisattva's practice—the accomplishment of Buddhahood. However, because of the unobstructed interpenetration of all phenomena—one of the basic themes of the sūtra according to the Hua-yen school—Buddhahood is the cause as well as the fruit of the Bodhisattva's practice. That is to say, the realization of the fruit of practice—the Buddha's enlightenment—is not only the goal of practice, but is also its supportive cause. In terms of the *Awakening of Faith*, the original enlightenment is the basis that supports the practice (or rather is what makes it possible at all), which in turn culminates in the realization of this original enlightenment that is inherent in everyone. So, from the perspective of the essential nature, the realm of practice (cause) is identical with the realm of realization (fruit). At the same time, from the point of conventional reality, the fruition of Buddhahood can only be realized after the consummation of the Bodhisattva Path, and thus, as Ch'eng-kuan says, the latter precedes the former.

This kind of understanding of the relationship between cause and fruit, practice and realization, is illustrated by the structure of the *Avataṃsaka Sūtra*. The sūtra opens with a majestic portrayal of the enlightenment site, and a beautiful description of the Buddha's enlightenment:

> At that time, the World-Honored One, seated on his seat, realized the most perfect knowledge of all dharmas. His wisdom entered the three times, equal in every respect. His body filled all worlds. His voice harmonized with all lands in the ten directions. Like space which contains the multitude of forms, he did not discriminate among all objects. Also, like space which pervades everywhere, he equally entered all lands. His body eternally sat at all sites of enlightenment. Amidst the congregations of Bodhisattvas his sublime light was effulgent like the arising of the sun disk, illuminating the world. The great ocean of his myriad blessings cultivated over the three times was already completely pure; yet he constantly appeared to be born in all Buddha-lands. His limitless body and his perfect light pervaded the whole *dharmadhātu,* equally, without distinction. He expounded all dharmas, like spreading out big clouds. The tip of each of his hairs could contain all worlds without obstruction, each displaying boundless preternatural powers, edifying and civilizing all sentient beings. His body pervaded the ten directions, and yet it had no coming or going. His wisdom comprehended all forms and realized the emptiness and quiescence of all dharmas. Among the miraculous acts of all Buddhas of the three times, there was none that was not completely seen in [his] light. The adornments of all Buddha-lands over inconceivable kalpas he caused all to be manifest.[40]

After this description of the Buddha's enlightenment and the rest of the introductory first chapter, in the early chapters the sūtra proceeds with the presentation of the fruit of Buddhahood, symbolized by Vairocana Buddha. This is done in order to "engender in the listeners a longing for and faith in the Teaching of the Buddha."[41] When, through seeing or hearing about the infinite wonders and perfect freedom of Buddhahood, faith has thus arisen in the future Bodhisattva, undertaking practice is the next natural step. Hence, after the fruit of Buddhahood has been revealed at the beginning of the *Avataṃsaka*, that is followed by an exposition of the practices and stages of the Bodhisattva Path, to which is dedicated the greater part of the *Avataṃsaka.*

According to Li T'ung-hsüan the depiction of the Buddha's enlightenment in the first assembly of the *Avataṃsaka Sūtra* represents the manifestation of Vairocana Buddha. On the other hand, the "Manifestation" chapter depicts the manifestation of the Bodhisattva's consummation of practice and understanding, wisdom and compassion, in his progressive cultivation of the stages of the Path.[42] Fa-tsang also states that after the previous chapters have explained the cause, this chapter demonstrates the fruit of Buddhahood.[43] Hence, the "Manifestation" chapter describes the final attainment of Buddhahood as a consummation of the Bodhisattva Path.[44]

Content Summary

The title of the "Manifestation" chapter directly introduces the main topic of the text. In Śikṣānanda's translation it consists of five Chinese characters. The first two characters (*ju-lai*) are the Chinese translation of "Tathāgata." Tathāgata is one of the epithets of the Buddha, and the two terms are often used synonymously. In Chinese the literal meaning is "Thus Come," or perhaps "One Who has Come from Suchness." The exact etymology of the Sanskrit word is not entirely clear. Besides "Thus Come," Tathāgata can also be interpreted as "Thus Gone," which is closer to the Tibetan translation of the term. In any case, a Tathāgata is someone who has come from and will return to suchness. Having realized his identity with the ultimate reality, he is the living embodiment of it. The next two characters in the title (*ch'u-hsien*) mean "manifestation" or "appearance." The last character is the Chinese word for chapter (*pin*). Thus I have translated the full title as the "Manifestation of the Tathāgata" (chapter).

According to Ch'eng-kuan's explanation of the title, found in his commentary on the *Avataṃsaka*, from the perspective of *dharmakāya* the meaning of Tathāgata is the suchness of all dharmas.[45] "Because the principle of suchness is always manifest, it is called 'manifestation.'" From the perspective of *sambhogakāya* he is called Tathāgata because, having practiced the True Path, he attained perfect enlightenment. In this case "the sudden simultaneous manifestation of the virtues of the original nature is called 'manifestation.'" From the perspective of *nirmāṇakāya*, "having assented to the vehicle of all-encompassing wisdom, he has come to edify sentient beings, and is thus called Tathāgata." Then his great function in response to others is called "manifestation." Thus, continues Ch'eng-kuan's explanation, "there is an ancient attainment by a new Buddha," and "a new attainment by an ancient Buddha."[46] Because it always responds to conditions, the true (*dharmakāya*) is the same as the provisional (*nirmāṇakāya*). Because the provisional arises dependent on the true, the provisional is the same as the true. Thus the three bodies (or three aspects of Buddhahood) are perfectly interfused. When one discerns the appearance of the provisional, that is also manifestation of the true.[47]

For the sake of easier reading and clearer presentation, in this volume's translation the "Manifestation" chapter has been divided into twelve sections. The original Chinese translation contains no such division; however, its contents and form do implicate such arrangement. The organization of the material reflects the *Avataṃsaka Sūtra* editors' predilection for classifying everything in categories of ten. The number ten figures predominantly throughout the *Avataṃsaka Sūtra*; it symbolizes infinity. Thus, Buddhahood is presented from ten perspectives, the expositions of which, together with the introductory and closing sections, constitute the twelve sections of the text.

The first section contains the introduction which provides the setting, and presents the main protagonists and subject to be discussed. The chief speaker, Samantabhadra Bodhisattva, is one of the two principal Bodhisattvas in the *Avataṃsaka Sūtra.* He represents the active aspect of Buddhahood, or its "cause"—the cultivation of the myriad practices of the Bodhisattvas. The name of the second main Bodhisattva in this chapter, Sublime Virtue of the Nature Origination of the Tathāgata Bodhisattva, signifies the teaching that is to be expounded.[48] According to Ch'eng-kuan, the word "nature" figuring in his name has two meanings: (1) "seed nature," which is the cause for the attainment of enlightenment, and (2) "Dharma-nature," the essential nature of things, which gives rise to both reality and phenomenal appearances.[49] Both of these meanings are related to the *tathāgatagarbha* (about which more will be said later). Other interpretations of this Bodhisattva's name, also mentioned by Ch'eng-kuan, point out that Sublime Virtue refers to Mañjuśrī. Mañjuśrī, the second principal Bodhisattva of the *Avataṃsaka Sūtra,* represents wisdom. The great wisdom of Mañjuśrī, explains Ch'eng-kuan, is that which can reveal, while the *dharmadhātu* of Samantabhadra is that which is revealed. When these two are joined together they become the manifestation of Vairocana,[50] the symbol of universal Buddhahood, which is the topic of this chapter.

The second section relates the characteristics and causes for the manifestation of the Buddha. The manifestation of the Buddha is dependent on the fulfilling of numerous causes and conditions. The intrinsic causes are the untiring cultivation of the Bodhisattva's attitudes and practices—the development of *bodhi-citta,* cultivation of compassion, kindness, wisdom, virtue, *samādhi,* taking of vows, etc.—as symbolized by the activity of Samantabhadra. The main external conditions are the influences from the Buddhas, especially their teaching of the Dharma which, though of a "single taste," is presented in numerous expedient ways in response to the abilities of the listeners. However, from the perspective of its essence, Buddhahood has no coming and going, it is formless, like space, not dependent on anything.

The next three sections elaborate on the physical, verbal, and mental activity of the Buddha. The body of the Buddha is presented as being immaterial and present everywhere. The Buddha is not to be perceived in just one person or one thing. The Bodhisattvas should perceive the body of the Buddha everywhere, in everything. While the essential body of the Buddha has no form and is impossible to grasp, yet for the sake of liberating sentient beings the Buddha manifests in the world and performs the unobstructed activity of universal salvation. Likewise, the voice of the Buddha is present everywhere. Pervading all sounds, it is ubiquitous, formless, without locus, beyond the reach of conceptual understanding. At the same time it constantly teaches sentient beings to abandon falsehood and cultivate the Path. Though the Buddha is impartial in his teaching and all his teaching has the same taste of liberation, due to the different capacities and mental attitudes of his listeners, his teaching is perceived differently. Likewise, Reality has a single undifferentiated flavor, and the "voice of perfect wisdom" is everywhere equal, but is heard in different ways by different people.

The mental activity of the Buddha is presented as *tathāgatajñāna*, the wisdom of the Buddha. *Tathāgatajñāna* is the foundation of all other kinds of wisdom, pervading them all. While all other kinds of wisdom arise dependent on it, *tathāgatajñāna* itself has nothing as support and does not increase or diminish. *Tathāgatajñāna* is equal, non-dual, beyond discrimination. It is fully present in the minds of all sentient beings, even though they are not aware of it due to their delusion and attachments. If beings, through the practice of the teaching, can let go of their delusions and attachments, then they will realize the infinite wisdom of the Buddha within themselves. This section contains the famous passage with the simile of a large sūtra contained in a particle of dust that affirms the presence of *tathāgatajñāna* in all beings. This is one of the most often quoted sections from the

Avataṃsaka Sūtra, and is among the clearest scriptural endorsements of the *tathāgatagarbha* doctrine.

In the sixth section the realm of the Buddha is presented as the knowing of the totality of the various realms. Further, it is also equated with the realm of mind, which is characterized as being boundless, neither bound nor freed.

The seventh section describes the activity of the Buddha as unlimited and unobstructed, without any abode. Their nature fundamentally quiescent, the Buddhas appear in the world to benefit sentient beings, without discriminating about doing so.

In the eighth section the enlightenment of the Buddha is described as reaching everywhere; it is also stated that it takes place in every thought of every sentient being. The Buddha's enlightenment is not taking place apart from the ordinary mind. Yet, while manifesting in the minds of all beings, the Buddha's enlightenment does not manifest anything. The enlightenment of all Buddhas is eternal and unchanging. Whether there are Buddhas accomplishing perfect enlightenment or not, the Buddha's enlightenment remains the same, neither increasing nor diminishing. The text also emphasizes that all of this is grounded on the understanding of the absence of self-nature in all dharmas. By realizing that all dharmas have no self-nature, the Buddhas accomplish enlightenment and continue to work for the welfare of all sentient beings.

The ninth section briefly recounts the turning of the Dharma-wheel, which symbolizes the teaching of the Buddha. The Dharma-wheel is not different from the speeches of all beings, because the reality of words and sounds is itself the Dharma-wheel.

In the tenth section the Buddha's Nirvāṇa is described as unoriginated, and hence not subject to extinction. From the perspective of the absolute the Buddhas neither manifest in the world nor enter Nirvāṇa, permanently abiding in the pure *dharmadhātu.* From the perspective of conventional reality, however, the Buddhas manifest in the world for the sake of benefiting sentient beings, and when their work is done they enter final Nirvāṇa.

The eleventh section extols the merits of seeing, hearing, and associating with the Buddha. It also contains injunctions to study the teaching presented and commends its efficacy. These are standard features often found in the closing sections of the sūtras.

The last section through a series of miracles communicates the universal significance of the teaching expounded. On a grand scale characteristic of the sūtra, it depicts the miracles that follow Samantabhadra Bodhisattva's exposition of the Dharma. As that happens in this world, so it is throughout all worlds in the universe. This is followed by the appearance of innumerable Buddhas, each of them called Samantabhadra, who shower praise on Samantabhadra and declare their intention to protect and preserve this Dharma. Samantabhadra Bodhisattva also receives praise from innumerable Bodhisattvas, each of whom is also called Samantabhadra, who come from innumerable lands in order to testify to him.

Related Doctrines

In order to gain better understanding of the teaching of the "Manifestation" chapter it is useful to get acquainted with some of the doctrines that are closely associated with it. From Indian provenance there is the *tathāgatagarbha* doctrine, for which the present text is one of the main scriptural authorities, and the doctrines of nature origination and conditioned origination, both of which were originated in China by the Hua-yen school on the basis of the teachings of the *Avataṃsaka.*

Tathāgatagarbha. The early origins of the *tathāgatagarbha* doctrine as a separate system of thought are not very clear. There are passages that echo its basic tenets scattered throughout the earliest parts of the canon. An often-quoted example from the Pāli canon is the passage from the *Aṇguttara-nikāya*, where the Buddha is recorded as saying: "This mind, monks, is luminous, but it is defiled by taints that come from without...That mind, monks, is luminous, but it is cleansed of taints that come from without."[51] Together with such sūtras as the *Śrīmāla*, the *Tathāgatagarbha*, the *Nirvāṇa,* and the *Perfect Enlightenment Sūtra*, and *śāstras* as the *Ratnagotravibhāga*, the *Fo-hsing lun (Buddha-nature Treatise*), and the *Awakening of Faith*, the "Manifestation" chapter is the most authoritative statement on this important Mahāyāna doctrine. The *tathāgatagarbha* doctrine exemplifies an ancient tendency in Buddhism to describe reality in positive terms. The *tathāgatagarbha* represents suchness (*tathatā*) manifest among defilements. It is conceived of as an indestructible luminous essence present in all sentient beings, which is the cause for their attainment of Buddhahood. This luminous essence, or "seed," is described as being neither existent nor non-existent. Sometimes it is spoken of as Buddha-nature, the True Mind, the mind ground, etc. It is also described as the suchness of things, their essential nature, or when spoken of in more apophatic terms, their emptiness. According to certain definitions, the *tathāgatagarbha* is also comprehended as the cause, or origin, of all pure and impure dharmas. In this sense it can be identified with the One Mind, about which Ch'an Master Huang-po (d. 850) has said, "All Buddhas and all sentient beings are only One Mind."

The *tathāgatagarbha* doctrine asserts that all sentient beings are endowed with the luminous True Mind of suchness, which is fundamentally enlightened and pure by nature. However, due to the generating force of ignorance this mind is covered with defilements, and thus cannot be perceived by unenlightened beings. Therefore, in *tathāgatagarbha* thought as understood in China, religious cultivation has as its goal the realization of this

True Mind, which is all there truly is from the very beginning. Instead of trying to radically transform the mind, one has to remove the defilements that cover it—or, according to certain systems of thought, to simply perceive their empty nature—thus allowing the primordial True Mind to manifest itself in all its purity and perfection.

Tsung-mi (780–841), the reputed fifth patriarch of the Hua-yen school, placed the *tathāgatagarbha* doctrine to the highest position in his taxonomy of the Buddhist teachings. In his *Ch'an-yüan chu ch'üan-chi tou-hsü* (*Preface to the Collection of All Explanations on the Source of Ch'an*) he identifies it as the "teaching which reveals the identity of the true mind with the nature." He explains it as follows:

> This teaching says that all sentient beings possess the true mind of emptiness and quiescence, whose nature is without inception fundamentally pure. Bright, unobscured, astute, and constantly aware, it constantly abides to the end of time. It is called Buddha-nature; it is also called *tathāgatagarbha* and mind-ground. [Because] from time without beginning it has been concealed by false thoughts, [sentient beings] cannot realize it, and thereby experience birth and death. The Supremely Enlightened, feeling pity for them, manifests in the world to proclaim that all dharmas characterized by birth and death are empty, and to reveal the complete identity of this mind with all Buddhas.[52]

Tsung-mi continues his explanation of the *tathāgatagarbha* teaching by quoting and explaining the already mentioned passage from the "Manifestation" chapter, which is said to contain the essence of the Buddha's message. This passage has often been used as a scriptural endorsement of the *tathāgatagarbha* doctrine:

> There is no place where the wisdom of the Tathāgata does not reach. Wherefore? There is not a single sentient being that is not fully possessed of the wisdom of the Tathāgata. It is only due to

> their false thinking, fallacies, and attachments that beings fail to realize this. If they could only abandon their false thoughts, then the all-encompassing wisdom, the spontaneous wisdom, and the unobstructed wisdom will clearly manifest themselves.... Children of the Buddha, the wisdom of the Tathāgata is also thus—boundless and unobstructed, universally able to benefit all sentient beings, it is fully present within the bodies of sentient beings. But those who are ignorant, prone to false thinking and attachments, do not know this, are not aware of it, and thus do not obtain benefit. Then the Tathāgata, with his unobstructed pure eye of wisdom, universally beholds all sentient beings in the *dharmadhātu*, and says: "Strange! How Strange! How can it be that although all sentient beings are fully possessed of the wisdom of the Tathāgata, because of their ignorance and confusion, they neither know nor see that? I should teach them the Noble Path, thus enabling them to forever leave false thoughts and attachments, and perceive the vast wisdom of the Tathāgata within themselves, not different from the Buddhas'." Having taught them how to cultivate the Noble Path so that they can forsake false thinking, after they forsake false thinking, they will realize the limitless wisdom of the Tathāgata, thereby benefiting and comforting all sentient beings.[53]

This passage has often been quoted and commented upon, and is perhaps the best known passage in the *Avataṃsaka*. Its direct disclosure of the presence of the Buddha's wisdom (*tathāgatajñāna*) in the minds of sentient beings had great appeal to the followers of the Ch'an school. The Ch'an teaching of "Mind is Buddha" was very much inspired by its tenor, and there are stirring records about the inspiration derived from its propitious message, as well as its role in providing a meaningful rationale for the process of practice and the actual experience that follows its sincere application.[54]

Nature Origination. The important Hua-yen doctrine of nature origination (*gotra-saṃbhava*) is closely related to the *tathāgata-*

garbha doctrine. It can even be said that nature origination is a Hua-yen appropriation of the *tathāgatagarbha* doctrine as the latter was understood in China. This assertion is supported by Fa-tsang's treatment of nature origination in his commentary on the *Awakening of Faith.* There he identifies nature origination as the unobstructed interfusion of the principle and phenomena, and places it under the rubric of "nature origination of the *tathāgatagarbha.*"[55] The nature origination doctrine was first developed by Chih-yen and is regularly utilized in the exegesis of the "Manifestation" chapter. In his sub-commentary to Ch'eng-kuan's commentary to the "Practices and Vows of Samantabhadra" chapter of Prajñā's translation of the *Avataṃsaka,* the *Hua-yen ching hsing yüan p'in shu ch'ao,* Tsung-mi explains nature origination in the following manner:

> There is not a single dharma that is not manifestation of the fundamental mind; there is not a single dharma that is not conditionally originated from the realm of reality (*chen-chieh*);[56] there is not a single dharma that is prior to the *dharmadhātu.* Therefore, the initial origination of the myriad dharmas is dependent on the realm of reality.... [In the compound] nature origination, "nature" corresponds to the realm of reality in the first sentence above, while "origination" corresponds to the myriad dharmas in the second sentence above. That is to say, the entire essence of the nature of the *dharmadhātu* originates all dharmas. Because the teaching of the dharma characteristics (*dharma-lakṣaṇa*) conceives of suchness (*tathatā*) as being congealed and immutable, it does not contain the principle of nature origination.[57] Because in this teaching[58] the true nature is transparent, mysterious, and bright, its entire essence being [its] function, it is naturally always the myriad dharmas. Because it is naturally always quiescent, its quiescence being the entire quiescence of the myriad dharmas, therefore it is not like the folly of nihilistic emptiness. Moreover, because the myriad dharmas are entirely quiescent myriad dharmas, it is not like the inverted view of regarding the seeming as the real,

> which is obstructed by its reification of things, embracing their distinctiveness and substantiality. Since all mundane and trans-mundane dharmas are entirely nature originated, there is no dharma outside the nature. Therefore all Buddhas and sentient beings mutually interpenetrate, pure lands and defiled lands are harmoniously interfused, the self and other of each dharma are mutually interconnected, and each particle of dust contains the universe.[59]

Fa-tsang similarly interprets nature origination as "arising of function dependent on the nature."[60] According to him the myriad phenomena arise from the nature, which is the way things always are, the suchness of things, when the nature follows conditions.[61] Nature origination thus means that all phenomena are ultimately based on the nature, which is the ultimate source of all mundane and supramundane phenomena in the universe. Therefore, it is said that all Buddhas and all sentient beings arise from the nature.[62]

It needs to be pointed out, however, that the purport of the nature origination doctrine is not to posit a certain absolute which is the ontological ground of the phenomenal realm, as it is sometimes misunderstood. The "nature" has no substance of its own, it is neither existent nor non-existent. It is the universal nature "which is the absence of nature."[63] It can also be described as the ultimate reality, true suchness, emptiness, all of which are inconceivable, ineffable, beyond the realm of dualistic opposites, the full understanding of which belongs to the realm of direct trans-conceptual realization. It is precisely because things have no self-nature, i.e., are empty and arise dependent on conditions, that we can state that they are nature originated. Here we are not confronted with two distinct orders—absolute and phenomenal—in which the first gives rise to the second. The nature origination doctrine rather clarifies the relationship between the ultimate reality and phenomenal appearances, which is that of interdependency. To say that all dharmas are nature originated means that "there is no dharma outside of the nature."

This topic is lucidly presented by Fa-shun in his seminal treatise *Fa-chieh kuan-men*. In the second section of that work, where he explains the relationship between the principle and phenomena, the third heading is designated as "establishment of phenomena by the principle." Fa-shun explains:

> This means that phenomena have no independent substance [of their own]; they can be established only in dependance on the true principle. [That is so] because all [phenomena] are conditionally originated [and thus] have no self-nature, and because all phenomena are established from the principle of lack of [self-] nature.... All dharmas obtain their existence dependent on the *tathāgatagarbha*. Contemplate this![64]

If we change nature for principle, the meaning here again is that all phenomena are established on the basis of the nature. But this nature is not something outside of phenomena, which depends on it for their existence. This principle, or nature, is in all things—it is the real nature of things. Further, as Fa-shun explains in the next heading, because phenomena are empty, they can "reveal" the principle (which is the principle that phenomena lack independent self-nature).[65] If it were not for phenomena, there would be no way to discern the principle, which is fully manifest in all phenomena.

Conditioned Origination. Together with nature origination, the doctrine of the conditioned origination of the *dharmadhātu* is one of the hallmarks of Hua-yen Buddhism. The two doctrines are closely related. Both doctrines are concerned with explaining the origination from the *dharmadhātu*, and their differences are due to the different connotations of this important concept.

Dharmadhātu is one of the crucial concepts in Hua-yen

thought. It often appears throughout the *Avataṃsaka Sūtra*, and also figures prominently in the writings associated with the Hua-yen school. Despite its importance, however, often there is certain ambivalence about its precise connotations. Its multi-faceted meanings are often difficult to distinguish, and the text of the *Avataṃsaka* rarely offers any clue in that respect. The term is a compound of two words: "dharma" and "*dhātu*." Chih-yen interprets "dharma" in three ways: as "mental object," "self-nature," and "norm."[66] In his commentary on the *Avataṃsaka* Fa-tsang also gives three definitions of "dharma": "that which upholds the self-nature," "norm," and "mental object."[67] The original Sanskrit meaning of *dhātu* is "element," while its Chinese rendering (*chieh*) is usually translated as "realm." Fa-tsang also defines *dhātu* in three ways: as "cause," "nature," and "(that which is) differentiated."[68] Depending on the way its two components are defined, the whole compound can be read in several ways. If *dhātu* is defined as "cause" then the compound can be understood as the cause for the attainment of Buddha-hood, i.e., the pure luminous mind. If *dhātu* is taken to mean "nature," then *dharmadhātu* can be understood as the essential nature of things, or the underlying reality behind phenomenal appearances. Both of these interpretations are related to the *tathāgatagarbha* doctrine. In the third meaning of *dhātu* given by Fa-tsang, "differentiated," the emphasis is on the distinct identity of each and every phenomenon. The meaning of *dhātu* in this case is similar to Fa-tsang's third definition of dharma given above (that is, mental object). Then the whole compound can be understood to refer to the realm of mutual identity and interpenetration among all phenomena.[69]

In the first two senses—cause and nature—*dharmadhātu* is related to the origination of the phenomenal realm from the true nature (i.e., the *tathāgatagarbha*), which is elaborated in the doctrine of nature origination. In the third sense, it refers to the mutual relationship among all phenomena, which is elaborated in the doctrine of conditioned origination.[70] The last is the sense in which *dharmadhātu* is usually used in Hua-yen writings when the discussion is based on the perspective of the perfect teaching. In that case it corresponds to the *dharmadhātu* of non-obstruction between phenomena (*shih-shih wu-ai fa-chieh*).[71]

The doctrine of the conditioned origination was first employed by Chih-yen, and was further elaborated by Fa-tsang, who established it as one of the cardinal concepts in the philosophical system of Hua-yen. The doctrine of the conditioned origination of the *dharmadhātu* for Fa-tsang epitomizes the highest insight of the *Avataṃsaka*, and by implication the highest teaching of Buddhism, which he called the "perfect teaching."[72] According to this doctrine, based on the absence of intrinsic nature in all phenomena and their dependant origination, each phenomenon is seen as being determined by the totality of all phenomena of which it is a part, while the totality is determined by each of the phenomena that comprise it. Because of this, each phenomenon is determining every other phenomenon and is simultaneously being determined by each and every phenomenon. This feature of mutual determinacy, or interdependency, of all phenomena is sometimes translated as mutual identity. Moreover, according to this doctrine, not only are all phenomena interdependent, but they also interpenetrate without any hindrance. Every phenomenon "contains" every other phenomenon, and every phenomenon also "contains" the totality of all phenomena which interpenetrate in perfect freedom and non-obstruction.[73] When this is translated in terms of practice and realization, Fa-tsang says:

> Thus, from the mutual interpenetration of the six characteristics in the conditioned origination of the *dharmadhātu*,[74] there is the simultaneity of cause and fruit, as well as their mutual identity, complete freedom, exclusion, and conformity. The

> cause is the understanding and practice of Samantabhadra. With enlightenment, the fruit is the boundlessness revealed by the realm of the ten Buddhas. All this is elaborated in detail in the *Avataṃsaka Sūtra*.[75]

While Fa-tsang placed the doctrine of the conditioned origination of the *dharmadhātu* to the position of prominence in his system, other important Hua-yen figures emphasized the doctrine of nature origination in their exegesis of the *Avataṃsaka Sūtra*. This is especially true of Li T'ung-hsüan and Tsung-mi, both of whom placed greater emphasis on nature origination because of, in their opinion, its greater soteriological value. While conditioned origination of the *dharmadhātu* corresponds to the mutual non-obstruction between all phenomena, nature origination corresponds to the mutual non-obstruction between principle and phenomena (*li-shih wu-ai*). But mutual non-obstruction between all phenomena is only made possible because of the mutual identity and interpenetration of each phenomenon with the principle. Thus, while nature origination indicates that all phenomena are established from the nature, or rather *are* the nature, conditioned origination illuminates the relationship between all phenomena—their mutual interdependency. While every phenomenon is determined by every other phenomenon, it is simultaneously dependent on the nature, which provides the ultimate basis.[76] Thus conditioned origination can only be established on the basis of nature origination, and is simply an extension of it.

On Reading the Translation

A note on reading the text presented in the translation. The text abounds in similes which, while used solely for the sake of illustration and their full comprehension is not necessary for grasping the essential purport of the text, often utilize themes and motifs from ancient Indian cosmology and mythology with which the modern reader is most likely not going to be familiar. Based on a worldview that is at great variance with our own, and moreover is rather obsolete, the profuse use of symbolism and the numerous similes found in the text might be a source of difficulty to the modern reader unaccustomed to religious literature of this genre. However, provided one has the proper attitude, that does not necessarily have to serve as an impediment; after all, patience is an essential aspect of the correct attitude, and an integral part of the practice whose development necessarily has to precede any genuine understanding of the text!

As with all scriptures of the great religious traditions, the present text has a form and ambience of its own which do not lend themselves to cursory reading. It is meant to be read and reread, contemplated and meditated upon. When approached with the simplicity of an open, humble, and pure mind, with the passage of time the quiet perusal of the scripture challenges one's (primitive) beliefs about oneself and the world, and reveals new perspectives on reality that are forever shut to the selfish small mind entangled in its fantasies and illusions. Thus, the study of the text has potential for leading the reader closer to the comprehension of the practices and vows of Samantabhadra. And that is truly an invitation to follow all the enlightened ones on the journey to the rediscovery of our true nature—the common bond that binds us all together. As Li T'ung-hsüan nicely puts it in his commentary on the "Manifestation" chapter:

> This chapter is about one's own progressive cultivation. After the five stations [of the Bodhisattva Path] have been traversed, the principle and wisdom, the myriad practices and great compassion are fully consummated. Then that is the manifestation of one's own Tathāgata; it is the teaching of non-attachment of living in the world and benefiting sentient beings. This chapter is like the great ocean—the rivers of earnest effort (*prayoga*) of

the five stations flow back to the vast ultimate.... The sūtra says, "The water of the great ocean flows under the four continents and the eighty million smaller islands, so that all those who drill inevitably find water."[77] This simile clarifies that all sentient beings have the ability to investigate for themselves, because there is no one who is not endowed with the mind of the great ocean of the Tathāgata's wisdom. The sūtra also says, "Bodhisattva-mahāsattvas should know that within their own minds there is always the Buddha's accomplishment of perfect enlightenment."[78] This [statement] clarifies that all the Buddhas, Tathāgatas, do not accomplish perfect enlightenment apart from this mind. Further below it says, "So it is with the minds of all sentient beings—within each of them there are Tathāgatas accomplishing perfect enlightenment."[79] This clarifies that the essence of the minds of [both] ordinary people and sages is pure and does not differ. There is only ignorance or enlightenment, without the slightest separation between them. If only for an instant false thoughts are not produced, then the mind and objects are both gone. The nature itself is unborn, because when there is no attachment and there is nothing realized, that is the accomplishment of perfect enlightenment. Then, to vastly benefit sentient beings with this Dharma is the practice of Samantabhadra. The sublime wisdom that has no mind, nature, or principle, and differentiates the one vehicle and the three vehicles, the causes and results of [the realms of] gods and humans, and the karmic retribution of the evil paths is called Mañjuśrī. In accord with differentiating wisdom, unweariedly acting together and benefiting beings while knowing their abilities is called Samantabhadra. With great compassion rescuing all sentient beings is called Avalokiteśvara. To simultaneously cultivate and learn with these three [kinds of] mind is called Vairocana. When these minds become habitual, it is called freedom. When there is not a dharma that is not clearly comprehended, it is called non-obstruction. When wisdom responds in accord with abilities, pervading the ten directions,

> [its] nature neither going nor coming, it is called preternatural powers. At the beginning of the practice it is habitually complete. [Though] falsehood is produced for many *kalpas*, the sun of wisdom does not change. This is altogether not difficult—why not put it into practice? Even if you study it without attaining anything, the merit thus obtained will still surpass that of humans and gods. [But] if you have no faith and do not practice, how can you end suffering? The great meaning of this teaching of the fruit of Buddhahood of the manifestation of the Tathāgata is that the sublime principle of Mañjuśrī and the sublime practice of Samantabhadra are fully possessed by all sentient beings. Neither past nor present, the nature itself has one essence. In order to influence future students to practice in this way, I sincerely say that it is not far off, so do not create difficulties by yourself....The main thing is that you should always trust that the different spheres of all your physical, verbal, and mental activity are produced from the different spheres of the physical, verbal, and mental activity of the Tathāgata. They are all devoid of essence, nature, self, and person. [Because] they are conditionally originated from the uncreated self-nature of the *dharmadhātu*, fundamentally no place where their roots have been planted can be found. The nature itself is the *dharmadhātu*, without inside, outside, or between. It should be known and inquired into in this way. Whether you are contemplating yourself or others, it is the same essential nature, without self or anything belonging to self. By the means of the power of *samādhi* and wisdom, practice in this way. When you know for yourself, then contemplate the suffering of sentient beings. Then benefiting oneself and others is like the vast vows and practices of Samantabhadra.[80]

Finally, after fully elucidating the prodigious practices of the Bodhisattvas and the inconceivable realm of the Buddha, the sūtra brings the reader back to the very ground from which all sublime qualities of the unobstructed activity and comprehensive enlightened awareness spring forth—one's own mind. Behind the depth of thought conveyed both in the recondite teachings and rich symbolism of the *Avataṃsaka*, as well as in the teachings of the ancient masters who derived their abstruse theories from their immediate experience of the teaching of the sūtra grounded on their deep contemplations, one of the primary purports of the sūtra is to offer a fresh perspective on the possibilities open to humanity. And once those possibilities are acknowledged, the *Avataṃsaka* offers an unexcelled guide to the actualization of their potential. The spiritual journey, described in the sūtra in minute detail with great beauty, which culminates in the realization of the highest awareness accessible to humanity, starts in the simple act of awakening of faith. This faith comes from the Buddha-nature inherent in the human heart, and provides the light that leads one beyond the familiar realm of meaningless obsessions, illusions, and worldly sentiments to one's true abode—the boundless *dharmadhātu*.

It is its practical usefulness in providing inspiration and guidance to all those who have the maturity and wisdom to see beyond their self-imposed limitations and dedicate their lives to the highest good that makes the sūtra truly meaningful. The Buddha of the *Avataṃsaka*, glorious and inconceivable as he may appear to be, is truly very close to each of us. He is much closer than anything one can conceive of—pervading everything, there is no place that he does not reach. The realm of the Buddha is the very reality in which the drama of our existence takes place. That same reality manifests completely in the single thought of faith in the mind of each ordinary person. It is the fundamental reality from which unfolds the Bodhisattva Path, which is the cause for the accomplishment of the fruit of Buddhahood—fruit that has been there from the very beginning, imperceptible to those who lack the eye of faith.

Part Two

MANIFESTATION OF THE TATHĀGATA

Prologue

AT THAT TIME, [in the Universal Light hall,][81] from the white curl between his eyebrows,[82] the World-Honored One issued a great light called "manifestation of the Tathāgata,"[83] which was attended by innumerable hundreds of thousands of billions (*nayuta*) of *asaṅkhyas* of lights. That light illuminated all the worlds in the ten directions throughout the *dharmadhātu*,[84] circled ten times to the right, manifesting the boundless freedom of the Tathāgata, enlightening the numberless multitudes of Bodhisattvas, quaking all the worlds in the ten directions, extinguishing all the suffering of the evil paths, overshadowing all the mansions of Māra, disclosing all the Buddhas, Tathāgatas, sitting at their seats of enlightenment and attaining perfect enlightenment (*samyak-saṃbodhi*), as well as all the assemblies at the sites of enlightenment (*bodhimaṇḍa*). Having done all of that, the light circled the assembly of Bodhisattvas to the right, and entered the crown of the head of Sublime Virtue of Nature Origination of the Tathāgata Bodhisattva.[85]

At that moment, everybody in the assembly at the site of enlightenment was filled with jubilation; enraptured, they all thought: "It is truly extraordinary! Now that the Tathāgata issued this great light, it must be that he is going to expound the deep and profound Dharma."

Then, on the lotus seat, Sublime Virtue of Nature Origination of the Tathāgata Bodhisattva uncovered his right shoulder, kneeled down on his right knee, joined his palms, and single-mindedly looking toward the Buddha, he uttered the following verses:

> Born from the virtue of correct awareness, with great wisdom,
> Penetrating all objects, arriving at the other shore,
> Equal to all the Tathāgatas of the three times,
> Therefore now I respectfully pay homage.

Having already ascended to the shore of the formless realm,
Yet manifesting a body adorned with sublime marks;
He emits thousands of undefiled lights,
And totally destroys the armies of Māra.

All the worlds in the ten directions
He can cause to quake without exception,
Without appalling a single sentient being;
Such is the awesome preternatural power of the Well Gone.

Equal to the nature of space and the *dharmadhātu,*
He can abide steady like that;
All the numberless living beings
He causes to obliterate evil and eradicate defilements.

Having diligently cultivated ascetic practices for
numberless *kalpas,*
He accomplished unsurpassed enlightenment;
His knowledge unobstructed in all realms,
Of the same nature as all the Buddhas.

The Guide issued this great light,
Quaking all the worlds in the ten directions;
Having manifested boundless preternatural powers,
It returned and entered my body.

Able to learn the definite Dharma well,
Numberless Bodhisattvas have assembled here,
Inducing me to ask about the Dharma,
Hence I now entreat the Dharma-king.

Now everybody in this assembly is pure,
Able to liberate all worlds;

Their wisdom limitless, without defiling attachments,
Such exalted sages have all assembled here.

The sublime Guide who benefits the world,
His wisdom and effort boundless,
Now illuminates the great assembly with light,
Causing me to ask about the unsurpassed Dharma.

Who can fully elucidate the profound realm
Of the Great Sage as it truly is?
Who is the Tathāgata's eldest son in the Dharma?
Honorable Guide of the world, please reveal this to us.

At that time, the Tathāgata from his mouth issued great light called "unobstructed (*apratihata*) fearlessness,"[86] which was attended by innumerable hundreds of thousands of billions of *asaṅkhyas* of lights. That light illuminated all the worlds in the universe, circled ten times to the right, manifesting the boundless freedom of the Tathāgata, enlightening the numberless multitudes of Bodhisattvas, quaking all the worlds in the ten directions, extinguishing all the suffering of the evil paths, overshadowing all the mansions of Māra, disclosing all the Buddhas, Tathāgatas, sitting at the seat of enlightenment and attaining perfect enlightenment, as well as all the assemblies at the sites of enlightenment. Having done all of that, the light circled the assembly of Bodhisattvas to the right, and entered the mouth of Samantabhadra Bodhisattva-mahāsattva.[87] After the light entered into him, the body and lion seat of Samantabhadra Bodhisattva surmounted hundredfold his original [body and seat], and the bodies and seats of all other Bodhisattvas, with the exception of the lion seat of the Tathāgata.

Then Sublime Virtue of Nature Origination of the Tathāgata Bodhisattva asked Samantabhadra Bodhisattva: "Son of the Buddha, the Buddha's display of supreme miraculous acts, which causes all the Bodhisattvas to rejoice, is truly inconceivable, unfathomable to [anyone in] the world. What is this auspicious sign?"

Samantabhadra Bodhisattva-mahāsattva said: "Son of the Buddha, when in the past I saw all the Tathāgatas, Arhats, Perfectly Enlightened Ones, displaying such supreme miraculous acts, they enounced the Dharma-teaching (*dharmaparyāya*) of the manifestation of the Tathāgata.[88] I reckon that the display of this sign indicates that this Dharma is going to be expounded." When [Samantabhadra Bodhisattva] said that, the whole earth quaked and issued countless lights asking about the Dharma.

Then Sublime Virtue of Nature Origination of the Tathāgata Bodhisattva asked Samantabhadra Bodhisattva: "Son of the Buddha, how should all Bodhisattva-mahāsattvas know the manifestation of all the Buddhas, Tathāgatas, Arhats, Perfectly Enlightened Ones? Please tell us.

"Son of the Buddha, all these countless hundreds of thousands of billions of Bodhisattvas assembled here have for a long time cultivated pure karma, and their mindfulness and wisdom is consummated; they have come ashore the ultimate supreme adornment, they comprise the dignified activity of all the Buddhas, they correctly recollect all the Buddhas without ever forgetting them, they contemplate all sentient beings with great compassion (*karuṇā*), they definitely realize the realms of preternatural powers of the Bodhisattvas, they are already supported by the preternatural powers of all the Buddhas, they are able to receive the sublime Dharma of all the Tathāgatas—replete with such boundless virtues, they have all assembled here.

"Son of the Buddha, you have already attended and made offerings to countless hundreds of thousands of billions of Buddhas, have consummated the unsurpassed sublime practices of the Bodhisattvas, have attained the freedom of all *samādhis*, have entered the arcane abode of all the Buddhas, you know all Buddhadharmas, have abrogated all doubts, are supported by the preternatural powers of all the Tathāgatas, you know the capacities of sentient beings and according to their predilections you explain to them the authentic Dharma of liberation in accord with the Buddha's wisdom, expound Buddhadharma, have reached the other shore—you are in possession of such boundless virtues. Excellent, son of the Buddha! Please expound the Dharma of the manifestation of the Tathāgata, Arhat, Perfectly Enlightened One, his physical marks, voice, mind, realm, practices, enlightenment, turning the Dharma-wheel, until his manifestation of entry into *parinirvāṇa*, and the wholesome roots (*kuśala-mūla*) begotten by seeing, hearing, and associating with him. Please explain all these things to us."

Then Sublime Virtue of Nature Origination of the Tathāgata Bodhisattva, wishing to once more enunciate the meaning of this, spoke the following verses to Samantabhadra Bodhisattva:

Excellent, you of unobstructed great wisdom,
Adroitly aware of the limitless realm of equality.
Please explain to us the boundless deeds of the Buddhas;
The children of the Buddha will be delighted to hear.

How should Bodhisattvas accord with and understand
The appearance of the Buddhas, Tathāgatas, in the world?
What are the realms of their body, speech, and mind,
As well as the ground of their activity—please explain all
of these.

How do all the Buddhas accomplish perfect enlightenment?
How do the Tathāgatas turn the Dharma-wheel?
What is the *parinirvāṇa* of the Well Gone?
The great assembly would rejoice to hear.

Those who see the Buddhas, great Dharma-kings,
And associate with them augment all wholesome roots;
Please tell us about their stores of merit,
And what do the beings who see them obtain?

If one hears the Tathāgata's name,
Whether he appears in the world or [has passed into]
Nirvāṇa,
If one awakens profound faith in his store of merit,
What are the benefits of that, please explain?

All these Bodhisattvas with their palms together
Respectfully behold the Tathāgata, you, and me;
The realm of the great ocean of virtues
Which purifies sentient beings, please tell us about it.

With anecdotes and similes,
Please explain the corresponding meaning of the sublime
Dharma;
When sentient beings hear, they will awaken the supreme
mind,
Their doubts obliterated and their wisdom pure as space.

Like the adorned bodies of all the Buddhas
Manifested throughout all lands,
With sublime voices, anecdotes and similes,
Please reveal the bodhi of the Buddhas like that.

In the myriad Buddha-lands of the ten directions,
For innumerable billions of *kalpas,*
An assembly of Bodhisattvas like this,
In all of them is rare to see.

These Bodhisattvas are all reverential,
Filled with esteem for the subtle meaning;
Please, with a pure mind fully elucidate
The vast Dharma of the manifestation of the Tathāgata.

The Characteristics of the Manifestation of the Tathāgata

At that time Samantabhadra Bodhisattva-mahāsattva told Sublime Virtue of Nature Origination of the Tathāgata Bodhisattva and all other Bodhisattvas in the great assembly: "Children of the Buddha, this is inconceivable. That is to say, the manifestation of the Tathāgata, Arhat, Perfectly Enlightened One, is accomplished because of infinite dharmas. Whence? It is not due to one condition, to one phenomenon, that the manifestation of the Tathāgata is accomplished; it is accomplished by ten boundless *asaṇkhyas* of phenomena. What are the ten? It is accomplished by the boundless *bodhicitta* that embraced all sentient beings in the past. It is accomplished by the past boundless pure superior aspiration. It is accomplished by the past boundless great kindness (*maitrī*) and great compassion that liberated and protected all sentient beings. It is accomplished by the past boundless continual practices (*caryā*) and vows (*praṇidhāna*). It is accomplished by the past boundless untiring cultivation of all blessings (*puṇya*) and wisdom. It is accomplished by the past boundless offerings to the Buddhas and edification of sentient beings. It is accomplished by the past boundless pure ways of wisdom and methods (*upāya*). It is accomplished by the past boundless pure stores of merit. It is accomplished by the past boundless wisdom of the ways of adornment. It is accomplished by the past boundless realization of the meaning of the Dharma. Children of the Buddha, when such infinite *asaṇkhyas* of Dharma-teachings are consummated, one becomes a Tathāgata.

"Children of the Buddha, it is like the great universe (*tri-sāhasra-mahāsāhasra lokadhātu*) which is not formed by only one condition,[89] only one phenomenon, but is formed by numberless conditions, numberless phenomena. That is to say, the formation of great clouds, the pouring of rain, and the four wind-circles provide perpetual support.[90] What are the four? The first is called 'able to support,' because it can support the great waters. The second is called 'able to dehydrate,' because it can dehydrate the great waters. The third is called 'establisher,' because it can establish all places. The fourth is called 'adornment,' because adornments are aptly spread everywhere. These are all produced by the collective karma of all sentient beings and by the wholesome roots of the Bodhisattvas, enabling all sentient beings to receive benefits according to what is appropriate. Children of the Buddha, the great universe is formed by such boundless causes and conditions. Such is the Dharma-nature (*dharmatā*)—without producer or creator, without knower, nothing accomplished, and yet all those worlds are formed.

"The manifestation of the Tathāgata is also thus: it is not brought about by only one condition, one phenomenon. It is brought about by numberless causes and conditions, numberless phenomena. That is to say, hearing, receiving, and sustaining the great clouds and rain of Dharma from the past Buddhas is the cause for the creation of the four wind-circles of the Tathāgata's great wisdom. What are the four? The first is the wind-circle of great wisdom of *dhāraṇī* that remembers without forgetting, because it can support the Tathāgata's great clouds and rain of Dharma. The second is the wind-circle of great wisdom that engenders calmness (*śamatha*) and insight (*vipaśyanā*), because it can obviate all afflictions (*kleśa*). The third is the wind-circle of great wisdom of skillful dedication (*pariṇāmanā*), because it can consummate all wholesome roots. The fourth is the wind-circle of great wisdom which engenders various unvitiated adornments, because it effectuates the purification of the wholesome roots of all beings who have been edified in the past, and perfects the power of the Tathāgata's undefiled (*anāsrava*) wholesome roots. Such is the Tathāgata's attainment of perfect enlightenment, such is the Dharma-nature: without production or activity, and yet it is accomplished. Children of the Buddha, this is the first characteristic of the manifestation of the Tathāgata, Arhat, Perfectly Enlightened One. Bodhisattva-mahāsattvas should know it thus.

"Further, children of the Buddha, like when the great universe is just about to be formed, the rain called 'inundation' pouring from the great clouds cannot be taken in or sustained anywhere, except when the universe is about to form. Children of the Buddha, likewise the Tathāgata, Arhat, Perfectly Enlightened One, gives rise to a great cloud of Dharma that rains profuse Dharma-rain called 'consummation of the manifestation of the Tathāgata,' which those of the two vehicles with their inferior aspiration are unable to take in or sustain, with the exception of the great Bodhisattvas with their continuous mental power. Children of the Buddha, this is the second characteristic of the manifestation of the Tathāgata, Arhat, Perfectly Enlightened One. Bodhisattva-mahāsattvas should know it thus.

"Further, children of the Buddha, as the great clouds pour rain due to the power of the actions of sentient beings, which comes from nowhere and goes nowhere, likewise the Tathāgata, Arhat, Perfectly Enlightened One, by the power of the wholesome roots of all Bodhisattvas gives rise to the great clouds of Dharma and rains profuse Dharma-rain, which also comes from nowhere and goes nowhere. Children of the Buddha, this is the third characteristic of the manifestation of the Tathāgata, Arhat, Perfectly Enlightened One. Bodhisattva-mahāsattvas should know it thus.

"Further, children of the Buddha, just as all sentient beings in the great universe cannot know the number [of drops] of the profuse rain pouring from the great clouds, and would become demented if they tried to count them, with the exception of Maheśvara, the lord of the universe, who by the virtue of the power of his wholesome roots cultivated in the past discerns every single drop of water. Children of the Buddha, likewise the Tathāgata, Arhat, Perfectly Enlightened One gives rise to a great cloud of Dharma that showers profuse Dharma-rain, which cannot be known by all sentient beings, *śrāvaka*s, and *pratyekabuddha*s, and if they tried to comprehend it, their mind would surely become unsettled. It is only the Bodhisattva-mahāsattvas, lords of all universes, who by the power of their enlightened wisdom cultivated in the past can clearly comprehend every single expression and sentence in the minds of [all] sentient beings. Children of the Buddha, this is the fourth characteristic of the manifestation of the Tathāgata, Arhat, Perfectly Enlightened One. Bodhisattva-mahāsattvas should know it thus.

"Further, children of the Buddha, like when the great clouds pour rain, there is a great cloud of rain called 'able to extinguish,' because it can extinguish fires; there is a great cloud of rain called 'able to raise,' because it can raise [the level of] the great waters; there is a great cloud of rain called 'able to stop,' because it can stop the great waters; there is a great cloud of rain called 'able to create,' because it can create all kinds of *maṇi* jewels; there is a great cloud of rain called 'differentiator,' because it can differentiate [the worlds of] the great universe.

Children of the Buddha, the manifestation of the Tathāgata likewise gives rise to great clouds of Dharma that pour profuse Dharma-rain. There is a profuse Dharma-rain called 'able to extinguish,' because it can extinguish the afflictions of all sentient beings; there is a profuse Dharma-rain called 'able to raise,' because it can give rise to the wholesome roots of all sentient beings; there is a profuse Dharma-rain called 'able to stop,' because it can stop the deluded views of all sentient beings;

there is a profuse Dharma-rain called 'able to create,' because it can create all Dharma-treasures of wisdom; there is a profuse Dharma-rain called 'differentiation,' because it can differentiate the predilections of all sentient beings. Children of the Buddha, this is the fifth characteristic of the manifestation of the Tathāgata, Arhat, Perfectly Enlightened One. Bodhisattva-mahāsattvas should know it thus.

"Further, children of the Buddha, as the water rained by the great clouds has a single taste, [but] there are numerous variations according to where it rains, likewise the manifestation of the Tathāgata rains the Dharma-rain of great compassion that has a single taste, and yet the explanations of the Dharma in accord with circumstances account for numberless variations. Children of the Buddha, this is the sixth characteristic of the manifestation of the Tathāgata, Arhat, Perfectly Enlightened One. Bodhisattva-mahāsattvas should know it thus.

"Further, children of the Buddha, as at the time of the creation of the great universe, first are created the heavenly palaces of the realm of form (*rūpa-dhātu*), then are created the heavenly palaces of the realm of desire (*kāma-dhātu*), and then are created the abodes of humans and other sentient beings. Likewise, children of the Buddha, the manifestation of the Tathāgata first engenders the wisdom of all the practices of the Bodhisattvas, then it engenders the wisdom of all the practices of the *pratyekabuddha*s, then it engenders the wisdom of the practices of all wholesome roots of the *śrāvaka*s, and then it engenders the wisdom of the practices of the conditioned wholesome roots of other sentient beings. Children of the Buddha, as the great clouds pour rain that has a single taste, due to the differences in the wholesome roots of all sentient beings the palaces produced are not the same. [Likewise] the Tathāgata's Dharma-rain of great compassion, though of a single taste, does differ according to the capacities of sentient beings. Children of the Buddha, this is the seventh characteristic of the manifestation of the Tathāgata, Arhat, Perfectly Enlightened One. Bodhisattva-mahāsattvas should know it thus.

"Further, children of the Buddha, when the worlds are about to be formed, there is a great water created, which fills the great universe. Covering that water grows a great lotus flower called 'precious adornments of the merit of the manifestation of the Tathāgata,' whose lustre illuminates all worlds in the ten directions. Then, when Maheśvara and [the inhabitants of] the heaven of purity see that flower, they decisively know that in that *kalpa* such and such Buddha will appear in the world. Children of the Buddha, at that time arises a wind-circle called 'well-purified light,' which can engender all the heavenly palaces of the realm of form. There arises a wind-circle called 'adornment of pure light,' which can engender the palaces of the realm of desire. There arises a wind-circle called 'strong, dense, indelible,' which can engender the great and small circles of the peripheral mountains (*cakravāla*) and the iron mountains. There arises a wind-circle called 'apical,' which can engender the ten great mountains. What are the ten? [They are] Khadiraka, Ṛṣigiri, Fu-mo shan, Ta Fu-mo shan, Yugaṁdhara, Nimindhara, Mucilinda, Mahā-mucilinda, Gandhamādana, and Himālaya mountains. There arises a wind-circle called 'peaceful abiding,' which can engender the earth. There arises a wind-circle called 'adornment,' which can engender the palaces on the earth and in heaven, the palaces of the *nāga*s, and the palaces of the *gandharva*s. There arises a wind-circle called 'inexhaustible store,' which can engender all great oceans in the great universe. There arises a wind-circle called 'universal light store,' which can engender all *maṇi* jewels in the great universe. There arises a wind-circle called 'firm root,' which can engender all wish-fulfilling trees. Children of the Buddha, the water raining from the great clouds has a single taste, without differentiation—it is only due to the differences in the wholesome roots of sentient beings that there are various wind-circles, and due to the differences among the wind-circles, the worlds differ.

"Children of the Buddha, the manifestation of the Tathāgata is also like this: consummate with the merit of all wholesome roots, it issues a light of unsurpassed great wisdom called 'inconceivable wisdom of the continuation of the seed of the Tathāgatas,' which universally illuminates all the worlds in the ten directions, bestowing to all Bodhisattvas prophecies about their consecration (*abhiṣecana*) by all the Tathāgatas, attainment of perfect enlightenment, and appearance in the world.

"Children of the Buddha, within the manifestation of the Tathāgata there is a light of unsurpassed great wisdom called 'pure and taintless' which can engender the Tathāgata's undefiled boundless wisdom. There is also a light of unsurpassed great wisdom called 'universally illuminating,' which can engender the inconceivable wisdom of the Tathāgata's universal entry into the *dharmadhātu*. There is also a light of unsurpassed great wisdom called 'upholding the nature of Buddhahood,' which can engender the Tathāgata's immovable power. There is also a light of unsurpassed great wisdom called 'far-gone and indelible,' which can engender the Tathāgata's dauntless indelible wisdom. There is also a light of unsurpassed great wisdom called 'all preternatural powers,' which can engender the Tathāgata's wisdom of all unique characteristics [of a Buddha] and the all-encompassing wisdom (*sarvajña*). There is also a light of unsurpassed great wisdom called 'creator of transfigurations,' which can engender the Tathāgata's wisdom of the indestructibility of the wholesome roots created by seeing, hearing, and associating [with the Tathāgatas]. There is also a light of unsurpassed great wisdom called 'universal accord,' which can engender the Tathāgata's body of boundless merit and wisdom, benefiting all sentient beings. There is also a light of unsurpassed great wisdom called 'inexhaustible,' which can engender the Tathāgata's deep sublime wisdom which, according to that which it is enlightened to, causes the seeds of the three treasures never to be obliterated. There is also a light of unsurpassed great wisdom called 'various adornments,' which can engender the body of the Tathāgata embellished with distinguishing marks, causing all sentient beings to rejoice. There is also a light of unsurpassed great wisdom called 'indelible,' which can engender the Tathāgata's supreme life span, equal to the *dharmadhātu* and the realm of space, beyond all limitations.

"Children of the Buddha, the Tathāgata's single-flavored water of great compassion is without differentiation; [however,] because sentient beings' propensities diverge and their natures are each different, it creates various wind-circles of great wisdom, causing all Bodhisattvas to effect the Dharma of the manifestation of the Tathāgata. Children of the Buddha, all the Tathāgatas have the same essential nature; from the sphere of great wisdom they create diverse lights of wisdom.

"Children of the Buddha, you should know that from the single taste of the Tathāgata's liberation arise boundless inconceivable kinds of merit. Sentient beings think that all of these are created by the Tathāgata's preternatural powers. [But,] children of the Buddha, they are not created by the Tathāgata's preternatural powers. Children of the Buddha, it is impossible that there could be even a single Bodhisattva who without planting wholesome roots with the Buddhas could obtain even a small part of the Tathāgata's wisdom. It is only due to the power of the Tathāgata's awesome virtue that all sentient beings consummate the merit of the Buddhas. And yet, the Buddhas, Tathāgatas, have no discrimination. There is no becoming, no dissolution, no originator, and no activity. Children of the Buddha, this is the eighth characteristic of the manifestation of the Tathāgata, Arhat, Perfectly Enlightened One. Bodhisattva-mahāsattvas should know it thus.

"Further, children of the Buddha, the four wind-circles that arise with space as their support can sustain the water-circle. What are the four? The first is called 'peaceful abiding'; the second is called 'constant abiding'; the third is called 'ultimate'; the fourth is called 'solid.' These four wind-circles can sustain the water-circle, which in turn can sustain the earth, preventing her from disintegrating. Therefore, it is said that the earth-circle depends on the water-circle, the water-circle depends on the wind-circle(s), the wind-circle(s) depend on space, while space itself depends on nothing. And yet, though it depends on nothing, it enables the great universe to subsist.

"Children of the Buddha, the manifestation of the Tathāgata is also like this—dependent on the light of unobstructed wisdom (*apratiṣṭhitajñāna*) arise the four kinds of wind-circles of great wisdom of the Buddha, which can sustain the wholesome roots of all sentient beings. What are the four? They are the wind-circle of great wisdom of aiding sentient beings and bringing joy to all of them; the wind-circle of great wisdom of establishing the proper Dharma and causing all sentient beings to delight in it; the wind-circle of great wisdom of protecting the wholesome roots of all sentient beings; the wind-circle of great wisdom of consummating all methods (*upāya*) and penetrating the undefiled realm—these are the four.

"Children of the Buddha, all the Buddhas, World-Honored Ones, with great kindness liberate all sentient beings, with great compassion rescue all sentient beings, with great kindness and compassion benefit all. Great kindness and compassion themselves depend on great skill in means, great skill in means depends on the manifestation of the Tathāgata, the manifestation of the Tathāgata depends on the light of unobstructed wisdom, while the light of unobstructed wisdom depends on nothing. Children of the Buddha, this is the ninth characteristic of the manifestation of the Tathāgata, Arhat, Perfectly Enlightened One. Bodhisattva-mahāsattvas should know it thus.

"Further, children of the Buddha, like when the great universe is formed, it benefits numberless kinds of sentient beings, viz.: the beings living in water obtain the benefits of the water; the beings living on earth obtain the benefits of the earth; the beings living in the [heavenly] palaces obtain the benefit of the [heavenly] palaces; the beings living in space obtain the benefits of space.

"Likewise, the manifestation of the Tathāgata in various ways benefits numberless sentient beings, viz.: those who rejoice in seeing the Buddha obtain the benefits of joy; those who keep the pure precepts (*śīla*) obtain the benefits of pure precepts; those who dwell in all meditations, absorptions, and the [four] boundless [mental states?] obtain the benefits of the great supramundane preternatural powers of the sages; those who dwell in the light of the Dharma-teachings obtain the benefits of non-effacement of cause and effect; those who dwell in the light of nothingness obtain the benefits of the non-effacement of all dharmas. Therefore, it is said that the manifestation of the Tathāgata benefits all numberless sentient beings. Children of the Buddha, this is the tenth characteristic of the manifestation of the Tathāgata, Arhat, Perfectly Enlightened One. Bodhisattva-mahāsattvas should know it thus.

"Children of the Buddha, when the Bodhisattva-mahāsattvas know the manifestation of the Tathāgata, they know it as boundless, because they know it consumates boundless practices; they know it as vast, because they know it pervades the ten directions; they know it as having no coming and going, because they know it is dissociated from creation, abiding, and destruction; they know it as inactive, without any activity, because they know it is dissociated from mind, thought, and consciousness; they know it as incorporeal, because they know it is like space; they know it as equal, because they know that all sentient beings are devoid of self; they know it as inexhaustible, because they know that it permeates all lands (*kṣetra*) without depleting itself; they know it as non-regressive, because they know it will never evanesce till the end of time; they know it as indelible, because they know that the Tathāgata's wisdom has no analogy; they know it as non-dual, because they know the impartial contemplation of the conditioned and the unconditioned; they know that all sentient beings obtain benefits, because the dedication (*pariṇāmanā*) of the original vows (*pūrvapraṇidhāna*) is spontaneously consummated."

At that time Samantabhadra Bodhisattva-mahāsattva, wishing to once more enunciate the meaning of this, uttered the following verses:

> The Ten-powered Great Hero is equal with the unequaled,
> Like empty space, beyond comparison;
> His realm is vast beyond measure,
> With supreme merit, transcending the world.
>
> The merit of the Ten-powered is limitless,
> Inaccessible to conceptual thought;
> A single teaching of the lion among men
> Cannot be known by sentient beings for a million kalpas.
>
> If the lands in the ten directions were pulverized to dust,
> There might be someone able to count the number
> [of particles];
> The merit of a single hair of the Tathāgata
> Cannot be stated in a hundred trillion kalpas.
>
> Like a person trying to measure space with a ruler,
> Followed by someone keeping the count,

The limits of space cannot be ascertained—
The realm of the Tathāgata is also like this.

There might be someone able within an instant
To know the minds of sentient beings in the three times
For as many kalpas as sentient beings,
Still he would be unable to know the nature of a single
thought of the Buddha.

Like the dharmadhātu which pervades everything,
But cannot be apprehended as being everything,
The realm of the Ten-powered is also thus:
It pervades everything, and yet is not everything.

Suchness is dissociated from falsehood and eternally
quiescent,
Unborn, indestructible, universally ubiquitous;
The realm of all the Buddhas is also thus:
Its essential nature is equal, neither increasing nor
diminishing.

Just as the reality-limit has no limit,
Universally present in the three times, and yet not universal;
The realm of the Guide is also thus,
Pervading the three times without obstruction.

The Dharma-nature is uncreated and immutable,
Like space, originally pure;
The purity of the nature of all the Buddhas is also thus:
The fundamental nature is not nature, beyond existence
and nothingness.

The Dharma-nature is not within [the sphere of] verbalization,

Ineffable, beyond speech, eternally quiescent;
The nature of the realm of the Ten-powered is also thus,
It cannot be deliberated in any words.

Realizing the quiescence of the Dharma-nature,
Like a bird flying in air without leaving any traces;
By the power of the original vows manifesting physical body,
Displaying the Tathāgata's great magic transfigurations.

If one wants to know the realm of the Buddha,
He should purify his mind [so that it becomes] like space;
Forsaking false thoughts and attachments,
Having the mind unobstructed amidst all objects.

Therefore the Buddha's children should listen well,
With few similes I will explain the realm of the Buddha;
The merit of the Ten-powered is immeasurable,
For the sake of enlightening beings I will now briefly
outline it.

All the realms manifested by the physical,
Verbal, and mental activities of the Guide,
The turning of the sublime Dharma-wheel and his
parinirvāṇa,
All wholesome roots I will now relate.

Like when the worlds are first formed,
They cannot be created by [only] one cause and condition;
It is innumerable causes and conditions
That create this great universe.

Likewise the manifestation of the Tathāgata is
Consummated by boundless merit;

The mind's thoughts numerous as the lands' particles of
dust might still be known,
But the causes for the birth of the Ten-powered cannot be
fathomed.

As at the beginning of a *kalpa* the clouds start to rain
And create four kinds of great wind-circles;
The wholesome roots of beings and the power of the
Bodhisattvas
Establish this universe firmly.

Likewise the Dharma-cloud of the Ten-powered
Gives rise to the wind-circle of wisdom and pure mind;
All sentient beings who have dedicated in the past,
It universally guides them to obtain the unsurpassed fruit.

As the great rain called 'inundation'
Cannot be sustained anywhere,
Except when the worlds are about to form,
By the power of the great wind in clear space.

Likewise the manifestation of the Tathāgata
Universally showers Dharma-rain throughout the *dharmadhātu,*
Which cannot be taken in by those of inferior mentality,
With the exception of those with pure and vast minds.

As a profuse rain pouring in space,
That comes from nowhere and goes nowhere,
Without creator or receiver,
Naturally diffused everywhere.

Likewise the Dharma-rain of the Ten-powered
Has no coming and going, no creation;

With the original practices as its cause, by the Bodhisattvas' power,
All those with magnanimous minds can hear and receive it.

Like a profuse rain pouring from the clouds in the sky,
Nobody can count its drops,
Except the free lord of the universe,
Who through the power of his merit can apprehend them.

Likewise the Dharma-rain of the Well Gone
All sentient beings cannot survey,
Except for those who are free in the world,
Who see it clearly like looking at a jewel in their palm.

As a profuse rain pouring from the clouds in the sky
Can extinguish, can engender, and can destroy;
It can produce all treasures,
Differentiating everything in the universe.

Likewise the Dharma-rain of the Ten-powered
Extinguishes delusions, engenders virtue, destroys all views,
Produces all treasures of wisdom,
And differentiates all predilections of sentient beings.

As the single taste of the rain in the sky
Differs according to the places it rains;
Though the nature of the rain does not differ,
In accord with differences among beings it appears thus.

The Dharma-rain of the Tathāgata is not one or many,
Equanimous and tranquil, beyond discrimination;
Yet in response to the various differences among those edified,
It naturally appears in numberless forms.

As when the worlds are first established,
First are created the heavenly palaces of the realm of form,
Then the heavens of desire, then the human abodes,
While the palaces of the *gandharvas* are created last.

Likewise the manifestation of the Tathāgata
First engenders limitless Bodhisattva practices,
Then it edifies the *pratyekabuddha*s who delight in quiescence,
Then the *śrāvakas,* then sentient beings.

When all gods first see the auspicious lotus flower,
They know a Buddha will appear, and thereby rejoice;
From water, with the power of wind, the world is created,
So that palaces, mountains, and streams all come to be.

The great light of the Tathāgata's innate virtue
Aptly distinguishes the Bodhisattvas and gives them
  prophecies;
The essences of all spheres of wisdom are pure,
Each able to elucidate all Buddhadharmas.

As trees depend on the earth for their existence,
The earth depends on water in order not to disintegrate,
Water depends on wind, wind depends on space,
While space depends on nothing.

All Buddhadharmas depend on compassion,
Compassion in turn depends on means,
Means depend on knowledge, knowledge depends on wisdom,
While the body of unobstructed wisdom depends on nothing.

Like when the worlds are formed,
All sentient beings obtain benefits;

Whether living on earth, in water, or in space,
With two or four legs—all obtain benefits.

The manifestation of the Dharma-king is also thus:
It brings benefits to all sentient beings;
Whether seeing, hearing, or associating [with the Buddha],
All effect the relinquishment of delusions and vexations.

The manifestation of the Tathāgata is boundless,
It cannot be understood by those deluded in the world;
For the sake of enlightening all sentient beings,
Where there is no similitude, similes are told.

The Body of the Tathāgata

"Children of the Buddha, how should Bodhisattva-mahāsattvas perceive the body of the Tathāgata,[91] Arhat, Perfectly Enlightened One? Children of the Buddha, all Bodhisattva-mahāsattvas should perceive the body of the Tathāgata in limitless places. Wherefore? All Bodhisattva-mahāsattvas should not perceive the Tathāgata in [just] one dharma, one phenomenon,[92] one body, one land, one sentient being. They should perceive the Tathāgata everywhere.

"Children of the Buddha, like space which is present everywhere, whether there are forms or not, without reaching or not reaching there. Wherefore? Because space is immaterial. Likewise, the body of the Tathāgata is present everywhere, in all sentient beings, all dharmas, all lands, without reaching or not reaching there. Wherefore? Because the body of the Tathāgata is immaterial—it is for the sake of sentient beings that he manifests a body. Children of the Buddha, this is the first characteristic of the body of the Tathāgata. All Bodhisattva-mahāsattvas should perceive it thus.

"Further, children of the Buddha, though space is vast and formless, it can manifest all forms; yet space does not discriminate, does not engage in conceptual proliferation (*prapañca*). Likewise, because the body of the Tathāgata is completely illuminated by the light of wisdom, it causes all karma of the mundane and supramundane wholesome roots of all sentient beings to be consummated. And yet, the body of the Tathāgata does not discriminate, does not engage in false differentiation. Wherefore? Because from the very beginning all attachments and false differentiations have been permanently obliterated. Children of the Buddha, this is the second characteristic of the body of the Tathāgata. All Bodhisattva-mahāsattvas should perceive it thus.

"Further, children of the Buddha, as when the sun rises over Jambudvīpa numberless sentient beings obtain benefits. That is to say, it dispels the darkness and brings light, it dries out the humidity, it enables the plants and the trees to grow, the grains to ripen, it makes it possible to see through space, enables the lotus flowers to bloom, the travelers to see the road, the inhabitants to conduct their activities. Wherefore? Because the sun disk emits boundless light everywhere. Children of the Buddha, likewise the sun of the wisdom of the Tathāgata universally benefits sentient beings in limitless ways. That is to say, it obliterates evil and engenders virtue, destroys stupidity and brings wisdom, it rescues with great kindness, it liberates with great compassion, it promotes evolvement of the faculties, their powers, and the conditions leading to enlightenment *(bodhipākṣika-dharma)*,[93] it causes the awakening of profound faith (*śraddhā*) and abrogation of the impure mind, it enables one to see and hear [the truth] without effacing cause and effect, it enables one to obtain the heavenly eye and see the places of birth and death [of sentient beings], it makes the mind unobstructed without effacing the wholesome roots, it causes wisdom to cultivate clarity so that the flower of enlightenment will bloom, it causes the arising of the mind [set on enlightenment] and the accomplishment of the primigenial practices. Wherefore? Because the preternatural body of the Tathāgata's sun of wisdom emits boundless light, universally effulgent. Children of the Buddha, this is the third characteristic of the body of the Tathāgata. All Bodhisattva-mahāsattvas should perceive it thus.

"Further, children of the Buddha, when the sun rises at Jambudvīpa it first shines on Sumeru and the other great mountains, then it shines on the dark mountains, then the high plains, and lastly it shines on the whole earth. [But] the sun does not think: 'I will first shine on this, than on that.' It is only because the mountains and the earth have different elevation that there is sequence in the irradiation. Likewise, the Tathāgata, Arhat, Perfectly Enlightened One consummates the sphere of wisdom of the limitless *dharmadhātu*, perpetually emitting the light of unobstructed wisdom, which first shines on the Bodhisattva-mahāsattvas, equal to the great mountains, then it shines on the *pratyekabuddha*s, then on the *śrāvaka*s, then on sentient beings with decisive wholesome roots, revealing the great wisdom according to their mental capacities, and finally it universally shines on all sentient beings, including even those who are inveterate in fallacy, in order to create beneficial causes that in the future will enable them to reach maturity. But the light of the Tathāgata's sun of great wisdom does not think: 'I should first shine on the Bodhisattvas [with their] superior practices, and in the very end I will shine on those sentient beings who are inveterate in fallacy.' He simply emits the light, equally shining on everyone, without obstruction, without hindrance, without discrimination.

"Children of the Buddha, as the sun and the moon always appear and shine on [both] the high mountains and the deep valleys without any bias, likewise the Tathāgata's wisdom universally shines on all, without discrimination; in accord with the differences in the capacities and the predilections of all sentient beings, the light of wisdom displays various differentiations. Children of the Buddha, this is the fourth characteristic of the body of the Tathāgata. All Bodhisattva-mahāsattvas should perceive it thus.

"Further, children of the Buddha, when the sun rises, those beings that are born blind cannot see it due to their lack of sight. Although they have never seen the sun, nonetheless they obtain benefits from its light. Whence? Because of it they can know the periods of the day and the night and can avail themselves of clothing and food, making their bodies feel at ease, free from adversity. It is the same with the sun of the Tathāgata's wisdom: those born blind, without faith and understanding, who break the precepts and hold erroneous views, who support themselves by improper livelihood, because they lack the eye of faith, they cannot see the sun disk of the wisdom of all the Buddhas. Though they fail to see the sun disk of the wisdom of all the Buddhas, they are still benefited by it. Whence? Because the awesome power of the Buddha effects the effacement of their physical pain and their afflictions, which serve as causes for future suffering.

"Children of the Buddha, the Tathāgata has a light called 'accumulation of all merits'; has a light called 'universal effulgence'; has a light called 'pure and free effulgence'; has a light called 'emanating supremely sublime sounds'; has a light called 'understanding all speeches and bringing joy to others'; has a light called 'the realm of freedom which reveals the permanent obliteration of all doubts'; has a light called 'free universal effulgence of non-abiding wisdom'; has a light called 'free wisdom which universally obliterates all false differentiations'; has a light called 'emanating sublime voices according to needs'; has a light called 'emanating pure free voices, adorning the lands, and bringing sentient beings to maturity.'

Children of the Buddha, each pore of the Tathāgata emits thousands of lights like these. Five hundred of these lights universally illuminate all congregations of Bodhisattvas at the sites of the various Buddhas in the various lands of the upper regions, while the other five hundred universally illuminate those in the lower regions. When those Bodhisattvas perceive these lights, they for a time attain the realm of the Tathāgata, with ten heads, ten eyes, ten ears, ten noses, ten tongues, ten bodies, ten hands, ten feet, ten stages, and ten wisdoms, all of them pure. All stations and stages that have already been consummated by all those Bodhisattvas become purer upon perceiving these lights; all their wholesome roots are brought to maturity, and they advance toward all-encompassing wisdom. Those of the two vehicles have all their defilements obliterated. Those other beings who are born blind, their bodies already rapturous, their minds purified, pliant and composed, are thus capable of cultivating mindfulness and wisdom. Those beings who dwell in the hells and the realms of hungry ghosts and animals all obtain happiness. They are released from their suffering, after the ending of the present life to be reborn in the heavens or among humans.

"Children of the Buddha, all those sentient beings have no awareness or understanding of the causes and preternatural influences by which they are reborn here. Those born blind think: 'I am Brahmā, I am a manifestation of Brahmā.' At that time the Tathāgata, abiding in the *samādhi* of universal freedom, emanates sixty kinds of sublime voices, telling them, 'You are not Brahmā, nor are you manifestations of Brahmā, neither were you created by Sovereign Śakra or the guardians of the world (*lokapālas*). All this is due to the awesome preternatural power of the Tathāgata.'

"When those sentient beings hear this, by the Buddha's preternatural power, they all recollect their past lives and become enraptured. Because their hearts are enraptured, they spontaneously produce clouds of *udumbara* flowers, clouds of incense, clouds of music, clouds of robes, clouds of canopies, clouds of pennants, clouds of streamers, clouds of fragrant powders, clouds of jewels, clouds of lion pennants and crescent towers, clouds of songs and eulogies, clouds of various adornments, and reverentially offer them all to the Tathāgata. Whence? Because all these sentient beings have obtained pure eyes. [Then] the Tathāgata gives them prophecies about their attainment of *anuttara-samyak-saṁbodhi.* Children of the Buddha, in this way the sun of the Tathāgata's wisdom benefits those sentient beings who are born blind, effectuating their wholesome roots to reach full maturity. Children of the Buddha, this is the fifth characteristic of the body of the Tathāgata. All Bodhisattva-mahāsattvas should perceive it thus.

"Further, children of the Buddha, the moon has four unique unprecedented characteristics. What are the four? First, it eclipses the lights of all stars; second, with the passage of time it appears as waning and waxing; third, its reflection appears in all clear and still waters in Jambudvīpa; fourth, it is in front of everyone's eyes to see; yet, the moon does not discriminate, has no false differentiation.

"Children of the Buddha, the moon of the Tathāgata's body, likewise, has four unique unprecedented characteristics. What are the four? It eclipses all *śrāvaka*s and *pratyekabuddha*s, both those who are still learning and those who are beyond learning; in response to what is appropriate it manifests different life spans, some long and some short, yet the Tathāgata's body has no increase or decrease; it inevitably manifests in the *bodhi* vessels of sentient beings with pure minds in all worlds; all those sentient beings who see it think: 'The Tathāgata appears only in front of me.' According to their predilections it elucidates the Dharma to them, according to their stages it leads them to liberation, according to the ways they need to be edified it causes them to see the Buddha's body; yet, the body of the Tathāgata does not discriminate, has no false differentiation—all the benefits it produces are brought to ultimate conclusion. Children of the Buddha, this is the sixth characteristic of the body of the Tathāgata. All Bodhisattva-mahāsattvas should perceive it thus.

"Further, children of the Buddha, as Brahmā, the ruler of the great universe, can, by a way of small expediency, manifest his body throughout the universe, so that all sentient beings can see Brahmā appearing in front of them. Yet, Brahmā does not divide his body, nor does he have multiple bodies. Children of the Buddha, likewise all the Buddhas, Tathāgatas, do not discriminate, have no false differentiation, nor do they divide their bodies, or have multiple bodies, and yet in response to the propensities of all sentient beings they manifest their bodies, without thinking they manifest many bodies. Children of the Buddha, this is the seventh characteristic of the body of the Tathāgata. All Bodhisattva-mahāsattvas should perceive it thus.

"Further, children of the Buddha, like a supreme healer who has extensive knowledge of various medicines and incantations, and has at his disposal all the medicines in Jambudvīpa. Because of the power of his wholesome roots from the past, and because of the power of the great bright incantations which he uses as expedient means, when beings see him they are cured of their illnesses. When that great supreme healer perceives that his death is approaching, he thinks: 'When I die sentient beings will have no one to rely on. I should contrive an expediency.' Then the supreme healer concocts medicine and spreads it over his body, sustained by the power of the bright incantations, thus ensuring his body not to decompose or decay after his death, so that its semblance, sight, and hearing will be no different from before. In that way it is able to cure all illnesses.

"Children of the Buddha, likewise the Tathāgata, Arhat, Perfectly Enlightened One, unequaled supreme healer, has already consummated the medicine of the Dharma refined over boundless hundreds of thousands of billions of *kalpa*s. Having cultivated and learned all means, expediencies, and the power of the great bright incantation, he has reached the other shore, and is able to skillfully obviate the illnesses of the afflictions (*kleśa*) of all sentient beings. [The Tathāgata's] life span is over limitless *kalpa*s; his body is pure, without thought, inactive, tirelessly engaging in all Buddha activities. When sentient beings see him, all the illnesses of their afflictions are completely obviated. Children of the Buddha, this is the eighth characteristic of the body of the Tathāgata. All Bodhisattva-mahāsattvas should perceive it thus.

"Further, children of the Buddha, as in the great ocean there is a great *maṇi* jewel called 'Vairocana's depository of all lights.'[94] If any sentient beings come in contact with its light they become of the same color; if they see it, their eyes become purified. Wherever its light shines it rains *maṇi* jewels called 'delight,' which cause all sentient beings to leave suffering and obtain ease. Children of the Buddha, likewise the bodies of all Tathāgatas are great collections of jewels, are great wisdom-stores of all merits. If any sentient beings come in contact with the light of wisdom of the treasure of the body of the Buddha, they become of an identical appearance as the body of the Buddha; if they see it, their Dharma-eyes are purified. Wherever this light shines, it causes all sentient beings to be freed from the suffering of poverty, and finally to fully obtain the joy of the Buddha's *bodhi*. Children of the Buddha, the *dharmakāya* of the Tathāgata does not discriminate, has no false differentiation, and yet it can, for the sake of all sentient beings, perform the great Buddha activity. Children of the Buddha, this is the ninth characteristic of the body of the

Tathāgata. All Bodhisattva-mahāsattvas should perceive it thus.

"Further, children of the Buddha, as in the great ocean there is a supreme wish-fulfilling king of jewels called 'treasury of the adornments of all worlds'; replete with myriad virtues, it causes all calamities that befall sentient beings at the place where it is to be abrogated, and their wishes to be fulfilled. However, this wish-fulfilling king of jewels cannot be seen by sentient beings with little merit.

"The wish-fulfilling king of jewels of the body of the Tathāgata is also like this: called 'able to cause all sentient beings to rejoice,' all those who see it, or hear its name, or praise its virtues will be empowered to permanently leave the suffering and distress of *saṁsāra.* If all sentient beings in all worlds simultaneously single-mindedly wished to see the Tathāgata, it will enable them to see him, thus fulfilling their wishes. Children of the Buddha, the body of the Buddha cannot be seen by sentient beings with little merit, unless they are disciplined by the free preternatural power of the Tathāgata. If sentient beings by seeing the body of the Buddha plant wholesome roots and mature them, for the sake of their maturation they will be enabled to perceive the body of the Tathāgata. Children of the Buddha, this is the tenth characteristic of the body of the Tathāgata. All Bodhisattva-mahāsattvas should perceive it thus.

"Because [the Bodhisattvas'] minds are boundless, pervading the ten directions; because their activity is unobstructed, being like space; because they universally enter the *dharmadhātu*; because they abide in the true limit of reality; because they have neither birth nor death; because they equally abide throughout the three times; because they are eternally dissociated from all discriminations; because they maintain their vows till the end of time; because they adorn and purify all the worlds; because they adorn the body of each Buddha."

Then Samantabhadra Bodhisattva-mahāsattva, wishing to once more enunciate the meaning of this, uttered the following verses:

As space pervades the ten directions,
Whether with form or formless, existent or nonexistent,
In the bodies of beings and lands throughout the
three times,
Universally present without limitations.

Likewise the true body of all the Buddhas
Pervades all *dharmadhātus*;
Impossible to see or grasp,
But for the sake of edifying beings it manifests forms.

Just as space cannot be grasped,
Yet it enables sentient beings to perform their activities,
Without thinking 'What am I doing now,
How do I do it, and for whom?'

Likewise the physical activity of all the Buddhas
Causes all sentient beings to cultivate wholesome
dharmas;
Yet the Tathāgata has never discriminated,
'I have done various things for them.'

As when the sun rises at Jambudvīpa,
Its light completely dispels the darkness;
Mountains, trees, ponds, lotuses, and earth,
All various things obtain benefits.

Likewise the arising of the sun of all the Buddhas
Gives birth to and nourishes the wholesome practices
of humans and gods,

Forever effacing the darkness of ignorance so that they attain the light of wisdom,
And procure all resplendent joy.

As when the sunlight appears,
It first shines on the great mountains, then the other mountains,
Then it shines on the high plains and the whole earth,
Yet the sun has never discriminated.

Likewise the light of the Well Gone
First shines on the Bodhisattvas, then on the *pratyekabuddhas*,
And then on the *śrāvakas* and sentient beings,
Yet the Buddha fundamentally has no thought movement.

As though those born blind do not see the sun,
The sunlight benefits them too,
Enabling them to know the time and receive drinks and food,
To be always free from adversities, and set their bodies at ease.

Beings without faith do not see the Buddha,
Yet the Buddha bestows benefits on them too;
Learning his name and coming in contact with his light
Can even be the cause for the attainment of bodhi.

As the clear moon in the sky
Eclipses all stars and appears as waning and waxing,
Reflected in all waters,
In front of all those who behold it.

Likewise the clear moon of the Tathāgata
Eclipses those of the other vehicles, revealing the long and the short,
Universally manifesting in the water of the clear minds of humans and gods,
All of them assuming to be in front of them.

As Brahmā, while staying in his palace,
Is ubiquitous in all Brahmā realms in the universe,
Perceivable by all humans and gods,
Without really dividing his body to go to them.

Likewise the manifestations of the bodies of all the Buddhas
Are ubiquitous in all ten directions;
The bodies are countless, impossible to tell,
Yet there is no dividing of bodies and no discrimination.

Like a supreme healer with great skill,
The seeing of whom cures all illnesses,
Though his life has ended, due to the medicine applied,
His body performs his work just as before.

Likewise the most supreme healer,
Fully possessed of means and all-encompassing wisdom,
Manifests the body of a Buddha by ancient sublime practices,
The seeing of which effects the effacement of beings' afflictions.

In the sea there is a king of jewels
Which radiates boundless light;
Beings who come in contact with it become of the same color,
Those who see it have their eyes purified.

The supreme King of Jewels is also like this,
Those who come in contact with his light become
of the same semblance;
If anyone sees him, his five eyes are opened,
Pulverizing the darkness of sensuality and abiding in
the Buddha stage.

The wish-fulfilling King of Jewels
Gratifies all wishes;
That sentient beings with little merit cannot see it
Is not because the King of Jewels discriminates.

Likewise the Well Gone, King of Jewels,
Satisfies all longings;
That beings without faith do not see the Buddha
Is not because the Well Gone rejects them.

The Voice of the Tathāgata

"Children of the Buddha, how should Bodhisattva-mahāsattvas know the voice of the Tathāgata, Arhat, Perfectly Enlightened One? Children of the Buddha, Bodhisattva-mahāsattvas should know that the voice of the Tathāgata is present everywhere, because it pervades all infinite sounds. They should know that the voice of the Tathāgata, according to their predilections, causes all beings to rejoice, because it clearly elucidates the Dharma. They should know that the voice of the Tathāgata, according to their faith and understanding, causes all to rejoice, because their minds attain purity. They should know that the voice of the Tathāgata edifies without missing an opportunity, because none of those who need to hear it do not hear it. They should know that the voice of the Tathāgata has no creation and destruction, because it is like an echo. They should know that the voice of the Tathāgata is without a master, because it is created by the cultivation of all actions. They should know that the voice of the Tathāgata is exceedingly profound, because it cannot be fathomed. They should know that the voice of the Tathāgata is free from depravity, because it is born from the *dharmadhātu*. They should know that the voice of the Tathāgata has no discontinuation, because it universally enters the *dharmadhātu*. They should know that the voice of the Tathāgata is changeless, because it reaches the ultimate.

"Children of the Buddha, Bodhisattva-mahāsattvas should know that the voice of the Tathāgata neither has bounds nor is boundless, neither has master nor is without master, neither explicates nor does not explicate. Whence? Children of the Buddha, just as when the worlds are about to disintegrate, without a master, uncreated, they naturally produce four kinds of sounds. What are the four? The first says, 'You should know that the joy of the first absorption (*dhyāna*) relinquishes the depravity of desire and transcends the realm of desire.'[95] When sentient beings hear this they spontaneously attain the first absorption, abandon their bodies in the realm of desire, and are reborn in the Brahmā heavens.[96] The second [voice] says, 'You should all know that the joy of the second absorption,[97] devoid of feeling and reflection, transcends the Brahmā heavens.' When sentient beings hear this they spontaneously attain the second absorption, abandon their bodies in the Brahmā heavens, and are reborn in the heaven of light and sound (Ābhasvara).[98] The third [voice] says, 'You should all know that the joy of the third absorption is without deficiency and transcends the heaven of light and sound.' When sentient beings hear this they spontaneously attain the third absorption,[99] abandon their bodies in the heaven of light and sound, and are reborn in the heaven of universal purity (Śubhakrtsna).[100] The fourth [voice] says, 'You should all know that the stillness of the fourth absorption transcends the heaven of universal purity.'[101] When sentient beings hear this they spontaneously attain the fourth absorption, abandon their bodies in the heaven of universal purity, and are reborn in the heaven of extensive fruition (Brhatphala).[102] Children of the Buddha, these voices are without master and are uncreated: they only arise from the power of the wholesome karma of sentient beings.

"Children of the Buddha, likewise the voice of the Tathāgata has no master, is uncreated, is without discrimination, neither entering nor leaving. It is only by the power of the virtues of the Tathāgata that four kinds of prodigious voices are produced. What are the four? The first [voice] says, 'You should all know that all formations (*saṃskāra*) are suffering (*duḥkha*). There are the suffering of hells, the suffering of animals, the suffering of hungry ghosts, the suffering of lack of virtue, the suffering of grasping at "me" and "mine," the suffering of acting in unwholesome ways. If you wish to be born as humans or gods, you should plant wholesome roots. Once born among humans and gods, you will leave all states of woe.' When sentient beings hear this they abandon fallacy and cultivate all wholesome practices; leaving all states of woe, they are born among humans and gods. The second [voice] says, 'You should know that the many kinds of suffering of all formations are fiery like a ball of hot iron. All formations are impermanent (*anitya*) and subject to cessation. The unconditioned happiness of the quiescence of Nirvāṇa is utterly dissociated from all burning, obliterating the fiery vexations.' When sentient beings hear this they assiduously cultivate wholesome dharmas; in the *śrāvaka* vehicle they attain the acceptance of accordance with what they hear. The third [voice] says, 'You should know that the understanding of [those in] the *śrāvaka* vehicle is based on someone else's words and their wisdom is inferior. There is a superior vehicle called *pratyekabuddha* vehicle, where one awakens without a teacher.

You should all study it.' Those who rejoice in the superior path, when they hear this voice they abandon the path of the *śrāvakas* and cultivate the *pratyekabuddha* vehicle. The fourth [voice] says, 'You should know that there is still a superior path which surpasses these two vehicles. It is called the Great Vehicle, or Mahāyāna; it is what the Bodhisattvas practice, observing the six *pāramitās*, not terminating the Bodhisattva practices, not renouncing *bodhicitta*, going through endless births and deaths without aversion. Surpassing the two vehicles, it is called Great Vehicle, Ultimate Vehicle, Superior Vehicle, Supreme Vehicle, Preeminent Vehicle, Incomparable Vehicle, vehicle which benefits all sentient beings.' If there are sentient beings with great faith and understanding, with sharp faculties, who have planted wholesome roots in the past, who are supported by the preternatural powers of all Tathāgatas, who have superior predilections and are intent on seeking Buddhahood, when they hear this voice they awaken *bodhicitta*. Children of the Buddha, the voice of the Tathāgata does not come from the body or the mind, and yet it can benefit numberless sentient beings. Children of the Buddha, this is the first characteristic of the voice of the Tathāgata. All Bodhisattva-mahāsattvas should know it thus.

"Further, children of the Buddha, as echo is created by the means of mountain, valley, and voice, it is formless, cannot be seen, and does not discriminate, and yet it follows all speeches, likewise the voice of the Tathāgata is formless, cannot be seen, it neither has locus nor is without locus, but is only produced in accord with the predilections and understanding of sentient beings. Ultimately, its nature is beyond words and explication, and cannot be elucidated. Children of the Buddha, this is the second characteristic of the voice of the Tathāgata, Arhat, Perfectly Enlightened One. All Bodhisattva-mahāsattvas should know it thus.

"Further, children of the Buddha, as in all heavens there is a

Dharma-drum called 'awakening.' When all gods start acting intemperately, [the drum] produces a voice in the sky, saying, 'You should all know that all sensual pleasures are impermanent, unreal and false, subject to momentary change and dissolution. They only delude the unwise, inducing them to create attachments. Do not be intemperate, because those who are intemperate sink into the evil paths, and repenting afterwards will be of no avail.' When those intemperate gods hear this voice they become greatly anxious and afraid. They leave all the sensual pleasures in their palaces and go to the ruler of the gods to request the Dharma and cultivate the Path.

"Children of the Buddha, the voice from that heavenly drum has no master, is uncreated, it has no creation or cessation, and yet it can benefit numberless sentient beings. It should be known that in the same manner the Tathāgata, wishing to awaken all intemperate sentient beings, produces infinite sublime Dharma-voices: the voice of non-attachment, the voice of restraint, the voice of impermanence, the voice of suffering, the voice of absence of self, the voice of impurity, the voice of quiescence, the voice of Nirvāṇa, the voice of limitless independent wisdom, the voice of the indestructibility of the Bodhisattva's practices, the voice of the ground of ubiquitous effortless wisdom of the Tathāgata. These voices pervade the *dharmadhātu* and awaken [sentient beings]. When numberless sentient beings hear these voices they all rejoice and assiduously cultivate wholesome dharmas, each seeking liberation by their specific vehicle, viz.: some cultivate the *śrāvaka* vehicle, some cultivate the *pratyekabuddha* vehicle, and some practice the unsurpassed Great Vehicle of the Bodhisattvas. Yet, the voice of the Tathāgata does not dwell at any location and is devoid of speech. Children of the Buddha, this is the third characteristic of the voice of the Tathāgata. All Bodhisattva-mahāsattvas should know it thus.

"Further, children of the Buddha, Iśvaradeva has a goddess

called Virtuous Mouth. A single sound of her voice tallies with a hundred thousand kinds of music, each of them containing a hundred thousand different sounds. Children of the Buddha, it should be known that as the single voice of that lady Virtuous Mouth produces numberless sounds, likewise the Tathāgata with a single voice produces numberless sounds, reaching all sentient beings in accordance with their different mental dispositions, thus causing them to obtain understanding. Children of the Buddha, this is the fourth characteristic of the voice of the Tathāgata. All Bodhisattva-mahāsattvas should know it thus.

"Further, children of the Buddha, as Mahābrahmā Devarāja,[103] while in his palace, produces the Brahmā voice which can be heard by anyone among the inhabitants of the Brahmā heavens, without egressing their multitude. All inhabitants of the Brahmā heavens think, 'Mahābrahmā Devarāja is speaking to me only.' Likewise the voice of the Tathāgata is heard by everyone assembled at the site of enlightenment (*bodhimaṇḍa*), but the voice does not egress the congregation. Whence? Because it should not be heard by those who are not mature enough. Those who hear it think, 'The Tathāgata, the World-Honored One, is talking to me alone.' Children of the Buddha, though the voice of the Tathāgata has no creation or abiding, it can still accomplish all its tasks. This is the fifth characteristic of the voice of the Tathāgata. All Bodhisattva-mahāsattvas should know it thus.

"Further, children of the Buddha, as though the various waters have a single taste, because of the different vessels the waters differ, but still the water does not ponder or discriminate. Likewise, the sound of the Tathāgata's voice has a single taste—the taste of liberation—but because of the differences among the mind-vessels of sentient beings it [shows] numberless differentiations, and yet does not ponder or discriminate. Children of the Buddha, this is the sixth characteristic of the voice of the Tathāgata. All Bodhisattva-mahāsattvas should know it thus.

"Further, children of the Buddha, as the *nāga* king Anavatapta engenders great dense clouds over Jambudvīpa that shower seasonable rain everywhere, so that the various crops can sprout and grow, and all rivers, springs, and ponds are filled [with water]. Though this profuse rainwater does not come from the body or the mind of the *nāga* king, it still brings numerous benefits to sentient beings. Children of the Buddha, likewise the Tathāgata, Arhat, Perfectly Enlightened One, engenders the great clouds of compassion that shower the sweet dew of the unsurpassed Dharma throughout all worlds in the ten directions, causing all sentient beings to rejoice, to augment their virtues, and consummate all vehicles. Children of the Buddha, the voice of the Tathāgata does not come from outside, nor does it egress from inside, and yet it can benefit all sentient beings. This is the seventh characteristic of the voice of the Tathāgata. All Bodhisattva-mahāsattvas should know it thus.

"Further, children of the Buddha, as when the *nāga* king Mānasa wants to shower rain, he does not do that instantaneously; he first engenders great clouds that cover the sky, and then he waits for seven days so that all sentient beings can finish their work. Wherefore? Because that great *nāga* king is kind and compassionate, and does not wish to inconvenience all sentient beings. After those seven days have passed, he showers gentle rain, moistening the whole earth. Children of the Buddha, likewise when the Tathāgata, Arhat, Perfectly Enlightened One, wants to shower the rain of the Dharma, he does not do that instantaneously; he first engenders the cloud of the Dharma in order to mature sentient beings, wanting them not to be startled or frightened. Once they are mature, he ubiquitously showers the sweet dew of the Dharma, explicating the exceedingly profound, sublime, virtuous Dharma, gradually leading them to consummate the unsurpassed Dharma-flavor of the all-encompassing wisdom of the Tathāgata. Children of the Buddha, this is the eighth characteristic of the voice of the Tathāgata. All Bodhisattva-mahāsattvas should know it thus.

"Further, children of the Buddha, as in the ocean there is a great *nāga* king called Extensive Adornments. When he showers rain on the great ocean, sometimes he showers rain with ten kinds of adornments, sometimes with a hundred, sometimes a thousand, or sometimes rain with a hundred thousand kinds of adornments. Children of the Buddha, the water does not discriminate—it is solely due to the inconceivable power of the *nāga* king that those adornments appear in infinite variety. Likewise, when the Tathāgata, Arhat, Perfectly Enlightened One, explains the Dharma to all sentient beings, he sometimes explains it with ten different voices, sometimes with a hundred, or a thousand, or a hundred thousand, or sometimes with eighty-four thousand voices he explains the eighty-four thousand practices, up to, with boundless infinite distinct voices he explains the Dharma, causing all hearers to rejoice. The voice of the Tathāgata does not discriminate—it is only that all Buddhas on the completeness and purity of the exceedingly profound *dharmadhātu* can, in response to the needs of sentient beings, produce various voices, causing them all to rejoice. Children of the Buddha, this is the ninth characteristic of the voice of the Tathāgata. All Bodhisattva-mahāsattvas should know it thus.

"Further, children of the Buddha, as when the *nāga* king Sāgara (Ocean) wants to manifest the sovereign power of a *nāga* king in order to benefit sentient beings and cause them all to rejoice, he contrives a vast network of clouds stretching from the four quarters of the world up to the heaven of power over the production of others (Paranirmita-vaśavartin),[104] covering everything. Those clouds are of infinite different colors: the color of the light of the golden sands of Jambu river (*jambūnada-savarna*);

the color of the light of blue lapis lazuli (*virūdhaka*); the color of the light of white silver; the color of the light of rock crystal (*sphaṭika*); the color of the light of white coral crystal; the color of the light of carnelian; the color of the light of supreme treasury; the color of the light of red pearl; the color of the light of boundless fragrances; the color of the light of immaculate garments; the color of the light of clear water; the color of the light of various ornaments.

The network of such clouds, after it has spread over everything, emits flashes of lightings of various colors. That is to say, the clouds of the color of the golden sands of Jambu river emit lightings of the color of lapis lazuli; the clouds of the color of lapis lazuli emit lightings of golden color; the clouds of the color of silver emit lightings of the color of rock crystal; the clouds of the color of rock crystal emit lightings of the color of silver; the clouds of the color of white coral emit lightings of the color of carnelian; the clouds of the color of supreme treasury emit lightings of the color of red pearl; the clouds of the color of red pearl emit lightings of the color of supreme treasury; the clouds of the color of boundless fragrances emit lightings of the color of immaculate garments; the clouds of the color of immaculate garments emit lightings of the color of boundless fragrances; the clouds of the color of clear water emit lightings of the color of various ornaments; the clouds of the color of various ornaments emit lightings of the color of clear water; and so on, until multicolored clouds emit lightings of a single color, and single-colored clouds emit multicolored lightings.

"From those clouds also emanate various sounds of thunder, in accord with the minds of sentient beings, causing them to rejoice. There are such sounds like the singing of goddesses, like heavenly music, like the singing of *nāga* maidens, like the singing of *gandharva* maidens, like the singing of *kinnara* maidens, like the sound of an earthquake, like the sounds of waves and tide, like the roar of the king of animals, like the singing of marvelous birds, as well as numberless other kinds of sounds. After the thunders there arises a cool wind, gladdening the minds of sentient beings.

"Afterwards it starts to rain various kinds of rain, benefiting and comforting numberless sentient beings. Everywhere—from the heaven of power over the production of others down to the earth—the rain is not the same: on the great ocean it rains cool water called 'unceasing'; in the heaven of control over the production of others it rains various kinds of music, like flutes, called 'exquisite'; in the heaven of production of pleasure (Nirmāṇaratāya)[105] it rains great *maṇi* jewels called 'great effulgence'; in the Tuṣita heaven[106] it rains extensive ornaments called 'hanging topknot'; in the Yama heaven it rains big beautiful flowers called 'various ornaments'; in the heaven of thirty-three (Trayastriṃśat)[107] it rains many exquisite fragrances called 'pleasantness'; in the abodes of the four guardians of the world (*catur-mahārāja-kāyikas*) it rains precious heavenly garments called 'covering'; in the palace of the *nāga* king it rains red pearls called 'issuing light'; in the *asura* palaces it rains weapons called 'subduing enemies'; in the northern continent (Uttarakuru)[108] it rains various flowers called 'unfolding'; in other places, likewise, it rains differently according to the place. Though the mind of the *nāga* king is impartial, without 'this' and 'that,' because the wholesome roots of sentient beings differ, the rains also differ.

"Children of the Buddha, likewise, when the Tathāgata, Arhat, Perfectly Enlightened One, unequaled Dharma-king, wants to edify sentient beings with the correct Dharma, he first spreads clouds of bodies filling the *dharmadhātu*, which, in accordance with the predilections [of sentient beings] appear variously. That is to say, sometimes for sentient beings he manifests clouds of corporeal bodies; sometimes for sentient beings he manifests clouds of transfiguration bodies; sometimes for sentient beings he manifests clouds of power-supported bodies; sometimes for sentient beings he manifests clouds of physical bodies; sometimes for sentient beings he manifests clouds of bodies with distinguishing marks [of a Buddha] (*lakṣaṇa-vyañjana*); sometimes for sentient beings he manifests clouds of merit bodies; sometimes for sentient beings he manifests clouds of wisdom bodies; sometimes for sentient beings he manifests clouds of bodies whose powers cannot be derogated; sometimes for sentient beings he manifests clouds of dauntless bodies; sometimes for sentient beings he manifests clouds of *dharmadhātu* bodies.

"Children of the Buddha, with such boundless clouds of bodies the Tathāgata covers all the worlds in the ten directions. According to the different predilections of all sentient beings he manifests various kinds of refulgent lightenings, viz.: he manifests for sentient beings lightening called 'reaching everywhere'; or he manifests for sentient beings a lightening called 'limitless light'; or he manifests for sentient beings a lightening called 'entering the arcane Dharma of the Buddha'; or he manifests for sentient beings a lightening called 'reflective light'; or he manifests for sentient beings a lightening called 'light refulgence'; or he manifests for sentient beings a lightening called 'entering the gate of limitless *dhāraṇīs*'; or he manifests for sentient beings a lightening called 'right mindfulness impassive'; or he manifests for sentient beings a lightening called 'ultimately indestructible'; or he manifests for sentient beings a lightening called 'comfortably entering all destinies'; or he manifests for sentient beings a lightening called 'fulfilling all vows and causing everyone to rejoice.'

"Children of the Buddha, the Tathāgata, Arhat, Perfectly Enlightened One, after he has manifested such numberless lightenings, in accord with the predilections of sentient beings, he produces boundless *samādhi* thunders, such as: the thunder of the the wisdom of skillful awareness *samādhi*; the thunder of the resplendent immaculate ocean *samādhi*; the thunder of the independence of all dharmas *samādhi*; the thunder of the diamond-wheel *samādhi*; the thunder of the pennant of Sumeru mountain *samādhi*; the thunder of the ocean seal (*sāgaramudrā*) *samādhi*;[109] the thunder of the solar lantern *samādhi*; the thunder of the causing all beings to rejoice *samādhi*; the thunder of the inexhaustible store *samādhi*; the thunder of the indestructible power of liberation *samādhi*.

"Children of the Buddha, after the thunders of such numberless different *samādhis* have manifested from the clouds of the bodies of the Tathāgata, before showering the rain of the Dharma, he first manifests an auspicious sign that awakens sentient beings. That is to say, from the unobstructed vast mind of kindness and compassion he manifests the wind-circle of the great wisdom of the Tathāgata called 'able to effectuate the arising of inconceivable joy and ease in all sentient beings.' After the appearance of that sign the bodies and minds of all Bodhisattvas and all sentient beings are purified. After that from the cloud of the *dharmakāya* of the Tathāgata, from the cloud of great kindness and compassion, and from the great inconceivable cloud, it rains the rain of the inconceivable vast Dharma, purifying the bodies and minds of all sentient beings. That is to say, for those Bodhisattvas who are sitting at the site of enlightenment it rains profuse Dharma-rain called 'nondistinction of the *dharmadhātu*'; for those Bodhisattvas who are in their final rebirth it rains profuse Dharma-rain called 'Bodhisattva's play in the arcane teaching of the Tathāgata'; for those Bodhisattvas who are about to attain perfect enlightenment in their next life it rains profuse Dharma-rain called 'pure universal light'; for those Bodhisattvas who are at the stage of consecration it rains profuse Dharma-rain called 'adorned by the ornaments of the Tathāgata'; for those Bodhisattvas who have attained forbearance it rains profuse Dharma-rain called 'blossoming of the flower of the wisdom of the jewel of merit, not ending the immensely compassionate Bodhisattva practices'; for those Bodhisattvas who are at the stages of the [ten] abodes, the [ten] dedications, or the [ten] practices it rains profuse Dharma-rain called 'entering the profound teaching of manifestation of transfigurations and cultivating the Bodhisattva practices without respite and weariness'; for those Bodhisattvas who are at the beginning stage it rains profuse Dharma-rain called 'engendering the Tathāgata's practice of great kindness and compassion and liberating sentient beings'; for those who pursue the *pratyekabuddha* vehicle it rains profuse Dharma-rain called 'profound understanding of dependent origination (*pratītyasamutpāda*), eschewal of both extremes, and attainment of the fruit of indestructible liberation'; for those who pursue the *śrāvaka* vehicle it rains profuse Dharma-rain called 'slaying the foe of all afflictions with the sword of great wisdom'; for sentient beings who accumulate wholesome roots—both those who are settled and those who are not—it rains profuse Dharma-rain called 'able to cause the consummation of the various Dharma-teachings and create great joy.' Children of the Buddha, all the Buddhas, Tathāgatas, in accord with the minds of all sentient beings rain such profuse Dharma-rains, filling limitless worlds. Children of the Buddha, the mind of the Tathāgata, Arhat, Perfectly Enlightened One, is impartial and is not parsimonious with the Dharma; it is only because the capacities and predilections of sentient beings differ that the Dharma-rains appear to be different. This is the tenth characteristic of the voice of the Tathāgata. All Bodhisattva-mahāsattvas should know it thus.

"Further, children of the Buddha, it should be known that the voice of the Tathāgata has ten kinds of boundlessness. What are the ten? They are: boundless as the realm of space, because it reaches everywhere; boundless as the *dharmadhātu*, because there is no place where it is not present; boundless as the realm of sentient beings, because it causes everyone's heart to rejoice; boundless as all actions, because it explicates their results; boundless as the afflictions, because it obliterates them all; boundless as the speeches of sentient beings, because it enables them to hear according to their understanding; boundless as the understanding and the desires of sentient beings, because it universally contemplates their salvation; boundless as the three times, because it is without boundaries; boundless as wisdom because it differentiates everything; boundless as the realm of the Buddha, because it enters the *dharmadhātu* of the Buddha. Children of the Buddha, the voice of the Tathāgata, Arhat, Perfectly Enlightened One, consummates such infinite boundlessness. All Bodhisattva-mahāsattvas should know it thus."

At that time Samantabhadra Bodhisattva-mahāsattva, wishing to once more enunciate the meaning of this, uttered the following verses:

When the great universe is about to disintegrate,
By the power of sentient beings' blessings a voice
  proclaims that
The peacefulness of the four absorptions is devoid of
  any suffering,
Causing them upon hearing this to forsake all desires.

Likewise the Ten-powered World-Honored One
Engenders a sublime voice which pervades the
  dharmadhātu,
Divulging that all formations are suffering and are
  impermanent,
Leading others to permanently cross the ocean of
  birth and death.

As a valley deep in the mountains
Produces an echo to each sound,
Though it follows other's speeches,
Ultimately the echo does not discriminate.

Likewise the voice of the Ten-powered
Manifests according to beings' maturity,
Causing them to be disciplined and joyful,
Without thinking 'I am now teaching.'

As the heavenly drum called Awakening
Constantly resounds the sound of the Dharma in the sky,
Exhorting all intemperate gods,
So that on hearing it they forsake their attachments.

Likewise the Dharma-drum of the Ten-powered
Produces various sublime voices,
Enlightening all sentient beings,
So that they obtain the fruit of bodhi.

Iśvaradeva has a precious maiden
Whose mouth intones various kinds of music,
A single voice that can produce a hundred thousand sounds,
And each sound another hundred thousand [sounds].

Likewise the voice of the Well Gone
With a single utterance produces all sounds;
Differing according to everyone's nature and predilections,
When heard it causes effacement of the afflictions.

As King Brahmā intones a sound
Which causes all Brahmā gods to rejoice;

The sound reaches them alone, without egressing,
Each saying that only oneself hears it.

Likewise the Ten-powered Brahmā King
Utters a single word that fills the *dharmadhātu*,
Without leaving the imbued assembly,
While those without faith cannot receive it.

As the many waters are of a single nature,
Flavored by the same eight virtues,
Due to the differences among the lands and the vessels
they are in,
They appear to have many distinctions.

The sound of all-encompassing wisdom is also like this,
The Dharma-nature has a single undifferentiated flavor,
But the differences in the actions of all beings
Cause their hearing to differ.

The great nāga king Heatless
Showers rain over the whole Jambudvīpa,
Which enables all herbs and trees to grow,
But does not emanate from his body or mind.

Likewise the sublime voice of all Buddhas
Rains throughout the *dharmadhātu*, fully diffused,
Advancing the creation of goodness and the effacement
of all evil,
Without emanating from inside or outside.

As the nāga king Mānasa
Engenders clouds that do not rain for seven days,
Waiting for all beings to complete their work,

And then starts the rain, thus bringing benefits.

Likewise when the Ten-powered instructs,
He first edifies sentient beings and brings them to maturity,
After which he elucidates the exceedingly profound
Dharma,
So that the hearers will not be startled.

In the ocean the nāga Great Adornment
Rains ten kinds of rain with adornments,
Or a hundred, or a thousand, or a hundred thousand kinds;
Though the water has a single taste, the adornments differ.

Likewise the Consummate Elocutionist
Elucidates ten or twenty Dharma-teachings,
Or a hundred, or a thousand, up to infinitude,
Without conceiving of differentiation.

The most supreme nāga king Sāgara
Creates clouds that cover the earth;
Though everywhere the rain is different,
The nāga has no discriminating thoughts.

Likewise all Buddhas, Dharma-kings,
Spread clouds of bodies of great compassion throughout
the ten directions,
Different for each of the rains of all practices,
Yet they do not differentiate among them.

The Mind of the Tathāgata

"Children of the Buddha, how should all Bodhisattva-mahāsattvas know the mind of the Tathāgata, Arhat, Perfectly

Enlightened One? Children of the Buddha, the mind, thought, and consciousness of the Tathāgata are unobtainable (*anupalabhya*). It should be known that only because wisdom is boundless that one can know the mind of the Tathāgata.[110] As space is the support of all things, while space has nothing for its support, so is the wisdom of the Tathāgata (*tathāgatajñāna*) support for all mundane and transmundane wisdom, while the wisdom of the Tathāgata has nothing as its support. Children of the Buddha, this is the first characteristic of the mind of the Tathāgata. All Bodhisattva-mahāsattvas should know it thus.

"Further, children of the Buddha, as the *dharmadhātu* constantly effects all liberation of the *śrāvakas*, the *pratyekabuddhas*, and the Bodhisattvas, while the *dharmadhātu* itself has no augmentation or diminution, likewise the wisdom of the Tathāgata constantly effects all kinds of mundane and transmundane wisdom, while the wisdom of the Tathāgata has no augmentation or diminution. Children of the Buddha, this is the second characteristic of the mind of the Tathāgata. All Bodhisattva-mahāsattvas should know it thus.

"Further, children of the Buddha, as the water of the great ocean flows under the four continents and all eighty million smaller islands, so that all those who drill inevitably find water, while the great ocean does not discriminate, 'I create this water,' likewise the water of the ocean of the Buddha's wisdom flows into the minds of all sentient beings, so that if all sentient beings contemplate its sphere and practice the Dharma-teachings, they will attain wisdom and clear comprehension. Yet, the wisdom of the Tathāgata is equal, non-dual, without discrimination; it is only due to the differences in the mental activities of sentient beings that the wisdom they each attain is different. Children of the Buddha, this is the third characteristic of the mind of the Tathāgata. All Bodhisattva-mahāsattvas should know it thus.

"Further, children of the Buddha, in the great ocean there are four jewels, replete with boundless virtues, which can engender all treasures in the ocean. If these jewels were not in the ocean, then it would be impossible to find even a single jewel. What are the four? The first is called 'collection of jewels'; the second is called 'inexhaustible store'; the third is called 'abandoning blaze'; the fourth is called 'ample adornments.' Children of the Buddha, these four jewels cannot be seen by all ordinary people, *nāgas*, spirits, etc. Whence? The *nāga* king Sāgara, because those jewels are beautiful and well-formed, keeps them in a very secret place in his palace.

"Children of the Buddha, likewise the great ocean of wisdom of the Tathāgata, Arhat, Perfectly Enlightened One, has four jewels of great wisdom, replete with the boundless merit of blessings and wisdom, which can engender the jewels of wisdom of all sentient beings, *śrāvakas*, *pratyekabuddhas*, those at the stage of learning and those beyond learning, and all Bodhisattvas. What are the four? They are: the jewel of the great wisdom of skillful methods free from defiling attachments; the jewel of the great wisdom of apt distinction of the conditioned and the unconditioned; the jewel of the great wisdom of distinctly elucidating infinite dharmas without transgressing the Dharma-nature; the jewel of the great wisdom of unmistakably knowing suitable and unsuitable time. If the great ocean of wisdom of all the Tathāgatas did not comprise these four jewels, it would be impossible for even a single sentient being to enter Mahāyāna. These four jewels cannot be seen by sentient beings with tenuous blessings. Whence? Because they are placed in the arcane store of the Tathāgata. These four jewels of wisdom are even and unbiased, stainless and exquisite; they can universally benefit the multitudes of all Bodhisattvas, empowering them all to obtain the light of wisdom. Children of the Buddha, this is the fourth characteristic of the mind of the Tathāgata. All Bodhisattva-mahāsattvas should know it thus.

"Further, children of the Buddha, the great ocean has four great jewels of effulgent light spreading over its floor. They have the quality of being extremely hot, always able to imbibe the measureless vast waters of the numerous rivers, so that the great ocean does not increase or decrease. What are the four? The first is called 'sun treasury'; the second is called 'abandoning humidity'; the third is called 'flame light'; the fourth is called 'total consumption.' Children of the Buddha, if these four jewels were not in the great ocean, then everything, from the four continents of the world up to the highest heaven of [the realm of] form (Akaniṣṭha), would be inundated. Children of the Buddha, the light of the jewel 'sun treasury' shines on the sea water and transforms it into milk; the light of the jewel 'abandoning humidity' shines on that milk and transforms it into sour milk; the light of the jewel 'flame light' shines on that sour milk and transforms it into butter; the light of the jewel 'total consumption' shines on that butter and transforms it into ghee, like blazing fire, consuming it totally without residue.

"Children of the Buddha, the great ocean of wisdom of the Tathāgata, Arhat, Perfectly Enlightened One, likewise has four kinds of jewels of great wisdom, imbued with a boundless light of awesome virtue. When the light of these jewels of wisdom touches all Bodhisattvas, it causes them finally to attain the great wisdom of the Tathāgata. What are the four? They are: the jewel of great wisdom that destroys the waves of all scattered virtue; the jewel of great wisdom that removes all spiritual desires; the jewel of great wisdom of universal refulgence of the light of wisdom; the jewel of great wisdom that is equal to the Tathāgata, infinite and effortless.

"Children of the Buddha, when all Bodhisattvas cultivate all auxiliary practices, they raise boundless waves of scattered virtue which cannot be destroyed by the gods, humans, or *asura*s of any world. The Tathāgata illuminates those Bodhisattvas with the light of the jewel of great wisdom that destroys the waves of all scattered virtue, causing them to renounce the waves of all scattered virtue, concentrate their minds on a single point, and dwell in *samādhi.* He also illuminates those Bodhisattvas with the light of the jewel of great wisdom that removes all spiritual desires, causing them to renounce their attachments to the flavor of *samādhi* and to arouse immense preternatural powers. He also illuminates those Bodhisattvas with the light of the jewel of great wisdom of universal refulgence of the light of wisdom, causing them to renounce the immense preternatural powers they have aroused, and to take up the effectual cultivation of comprehensive understanding. He also illuminates those Bodhisattvas with the light of the jewel of great wisdom that is equal to the Tathāgata, infinite and effortless, causing them all to renounce the effectual cultivation of comprehensive understanding they have taken up, so that they will finally arrive at the impartial stage of the Tathāgata, ending all actions without residue. Children of the Buddha, if it was not for the great light of these four jewels of wisdom of the Tathāgata, it would be impossible for even a single Bodhisattva to attain the stage of Tathāgata. Children of the Buddha, this is the fifth characteristic of the mind of the Tathāgata. All Bodhisattva-mahāsattvas should know it thus.

"Further, children of the Buddha, the billion lands lying from the realm of water up to the heaven of neither thinking nor non-thinking, the abodes of all sentient beings in the realm of desire, the realm of form, and the formless realm, all arise dependent on space, and dwell in space. Whence? Because space is ubiquitous. But even though space contains all three realms, it does not discriminate. Children of the Buddha, the wisdom of the Tathāgata is also thus: whether it is the wisdom of the *śrāvakas*, or the wisdom of the *pratyekabuddhas*, or the wisdom of the Bodhisattvas, or the wisdom of conditioned practice, or the wisdom of unconditioned practice, all of these arise dependent on the wisdom of the Tathāgata, dwell in the wisdom of the Tathāgata. Whence? Because the wisdom of the Tathāgata pervades them all. But even though it contains all infinite wisdoms, it does not discriminate. Children of the Buddha, this is the sixth characteristic of the mind of the Tathāgata. All Bodhisattva-mahāsattvas should know it thus.

"Further, children of the Buddha, atop the Himālaya mountains there is a sovereign healing tree called 'limitless roots.' The roots of that healing tree grow from a hundred and sixty-eight thousand *yojanas*[111] all the way down to the diamond ground of the circle of water. When the roots of that sovereign healing tree grow, they cause the roots of all trees in Jambudvīpa to grow; when its stems grow, that causes the stems of all trees in Jambudvīpa to grow. It is the same with its branches, leaves, flowers, and fruit. The roots of this sovereign healing tree can produce stems, while its stems can produce roots. [Because its] roots have no limits, it is called 'limitless roots.' Children of the Buddha, that sovereign healing tree can grow everywhere, with the exception of two places, where it cannot render the benefit of its growth—the deep pit of the hells and the circle of water. However, it does not cherish dislike even for these.

"Children of the Buddha, likewise the great sovereign healing tree of the wisdom of the Tathāgata, by all virtues of wisdom initiated and consummated in the past, universally covers all realms of sentient beings and obliterates all sufferings of the evil paths. The vast vows of great compassion are its roots; the steadfast unmoving skillful methods born from the inherent nature of the true wisdom of all the Tathāgatas are its stems; the universal wisdom of the *dharmadhātu* and all *pāramitās* are its branches; meditation, liberation (*vimokṣa*), and all great *samādhis* are its leaves; complete control [over good and evil] (*dhāraṇī*), eloquence, and the conditions leading to enlightenment (*bodhipākṣika-dharma*) are its flowers; the ultimate immutable liberation of all the Buddhas is its fruit.

"Children of the Buddha, for what reasons is the great sovereign healing tree of the wisdom of the Tathāgata called 'limitless roots'? Because of being ultimately untiring, and because of not terminating the Bodhisattvas' practice. The Bodhisattvas' practice is the nature of the Tathāgata; the nature of the Tathāgata is the Bodhisattvas' practice. Therefore it is called 'limitless roots.'

"Children of the Buddha, when the roots of the great sovereign healing tree of the wisdom of the Tathāgata grow, that effects all Bodhisattvas to grow the roots of great kindness and compassion which do not abandon sentient beings. When its stems grow, that effects all Bodhisattvas to augment their stems of the profound mind of concentrated effort. When its branches grow, that effects all Bodhisattvas to augment the branches of all *pāramitās*. When its leaves grow, that effects all Bodhisattvas to develop the leaves of pure discipline (*śīla*), austerities, merit, exiguity of desire, and knowledge of contentment. When its flowers grow, that effects all Bodhisattvas to fulfil the flowers of the adornments of all wholesome roots and embellishing marks. When it bears fruit, it effects all Bodhisattvas to attain the fruits of acceptance of non-creation, up to acceptance of bestowal of consecration by all the Buddhas.

"Children of the Buddha, the great sovereign healing tree of the wisdom of the Tathāgata cannot render the benefits [arising from] its growth in only two places: in those of the two vehicles who have sunk into the exceedingly deep pit of the unconditioned, and in unfit sentient beings with impaired wholesome roots who have sunk into the vast waters of heterodox views and greedy attachments. However, it has not abandoned even those beings. Children of the Buddha, the wisdom of the Tathāgata has no increase or decrease, because its roots are firmly planted and it grows without respite. Children of the Buddha, this is the seventh characteristic of the mind of the Tathāgata. All Bodhisattva-mahāsattvas should know it thus.

"Further, children of the Buddha, at the time of the arising of fire in the *kalpa* of the destruction of the great universe, the raging fire entirely consumes all plants and forests, as well as everything else including the enclosing iron mountains (*cakravāla*)[112] and the great enclosing iron mountains (*mahā-cakravāla*),[113] burning them completely without residue. Children of the Buddha, if then a person were to throw a handful of grass into the fire, do you think that it could happen that it would not burn?"

"No."

"Children of the Buddha, it would still be possible for that grass not to burn, but it would be utterly impossible for the wisdom of the Tathāgata, which differentiates all sentient beings, all lands, all *kalpas*, and all dharmas in the three times, not to know something. Wherefore? Because that wisdom is equal, clearly penetrating everything. Children of the Buddha, this is the eighth characteristic of the mind of the Tathāgata. All Bodhisattva-mahāsattvas should know it thus.

"Further, children of the Buddha, at the time of the calamity of the destruction of the world by wind, there arises a great wind called 'devastation,' which can destroy all worlds in the great universe—including the enclosing iron mountains—reducing everything to tiny particles. There is also another wind called 'able to obstruct,' which circles around the great universe, obstructing the devastating wind, and thus not allowing it to reach the worlds of other universes. Children of the Buddha, if it were not for this obstructing wind, the worlds of the ten directions would be destroyed entirely. Likewise the Tathāgata, Arhat, Perfectly Enlightened One, has a great wind of wisdom called 'able to obliterate,' which can obliterate the afflictions (*kleśa*) and forces of habit (*vāsanā*) of all great Bodhisattvas; and a great wind of wisdom called 'skillful support,' which skillfully supports immature Bodhisattvas, not allowing the 'able to obliterate' great wind of wisdom to destroy all their afflictions and forces of habit. Children of the Buddha, if it were not for the Tathāgata's 'skillful support' wind of wisdom, then infinite Bodhisattvas would fall into the stages of *śrāvaka*s and *pratyekabuddha*s. It is by this wisdom that all Bodhisattvas are empowered to go beyond the stages of the two vehicles, and securely dwell in the ultimate stage of the Tathāgata. Children of the Buddha, this is the ninth characteristic of the mind of the Tathāgata. All Bodhisattva-mahāsattvas should know it thus.

"Further, children of the Buddha, there is no place where the wisdom of the Tathāgata does not reach. Wherefore? There is not a single sentient being that is not fully possessed of the wisdom of the Tathāgata.[114] It is only due to their false thinking, fallacies, and attachments that beings fail to realize this. If they could only abandon their false thoughts, then the all-encompassing wisdom, the spontaneous wisdom, and the unobstructed wisdom will clearly manifest themselves.[115]

"Children of the Buddha, just as if there was a great sūtra, as extensive as the great universe, in which are written down all phenomena in the great universe. That is to say, in it is written about the phenomena in the great enclosing iron mountains, as extensively as the great enclosing iron mountains; it is written about the phenomena on earth, as extensively as the earth; it is written about the phenomena in the medium universe,[116] as extensively as the medium universe; it is written about the phenomena in the small universe,[117] as extensively as the small universe. In the same vain, all phenomena—be they of the four continents, or the great oceans, Sumeru mountains, the palaces of the gods on earth, the palaces of the gods in the heavens of the realm of desire, the palaces in the realm of form, and the palaces of the formless realm—are written down to an equal length. Even though this sūtra is as extensive as the great universe, it can be fully comprised within a single particle of dust. As it is with one particle of dust, so it is with all particles of dust.

"Then a person with perfect wisdom, who has perfected the pure heavenly eye, seeing that great sūtra inside a particle of dust, without being of even the slightest benefit to all sentient beings, thinks, 'I should exert myself to break that particle of dust and take out the sūtra so that it would be of benefit to sentient beings.' Having thought thus, he contrives an expedient method to break the particle of dust and take out the great sūtra, thus enabling all sentient beings to obtain benefits. As he does with one particle of dust, it should be known that he does so with all particles of dust.

"Children of the Buddha, the wisdom of the Tathāgata is also thus—boundless and unobstructed, universally able to benefit all sentient beings, it is fully present within the bodies of sentient beings. But those who are ignorant, prone to false thinking and attachments, do not know this, are not aware of it, and thus do not obtain benefit. Then the Tathāgata, with his unobstructed pure eye of wisdom, universally beholds all sentient beings in the *dharmadhātu*, and says: 'Strange! How Strange! How can it be that although all sentient beings are fully possessed of the wisdom of the Tathāgata, because of their ignorance and confusion, they neither know nor see that? I should teach them the Noble Path, thus enabling them to forever leave false thoughts and attachments, and perceive the great wisdom of the Tathāgata within themselves, not different from the Buddhas'.' Having taught them how to cultivate the Noble Path so that they can forsake false thinking, after they forsake false thinking, they will realize the limitless wisdom of the Tathāgata, thereby benefiting and comforting all sentient beings.[118] Children of the Buddha, this is the tenth characteristic of the mind of the Tathāgata. All Bodhisattva-mahāsattvas should know it thus.

"Children of the Buddha, Bodhisattva-mahāsattvas should by such boundless, unobstructed, inconceivable, vast characteristics know the mind of the Tathāgata, Arhat, Perfectly Enlightened One."

At that time Samantabhadra Bodhisattva-mahāsattva, wishing to once more enunciate the meaning of this, uttered the following verses:

Those who wish to know the mind of all Buddhas,
Should contemplate the Buddha's wisdom;
The Buddha's wisdom has no support,
Like space which is supported by nothing.

The various propensities of sentient beings
And all expedient wisdom,
Each depends on the Buddha's wisdom,
While the Buddha's wisdom depends on nothing.

The liberation of all the *śrāvakas,*
Pratyekabuddhas, and Buddhas,
Each depends on the *dharmadhātu,*
While the *dharmadhātu* has no increase or decrease.

Likewise the Buddha's wisdom
Engenders all wisdom,
Without increase or decrease,
Unborn and inexhaustible.

As the water flows under the earth,
To be found by all those who look for it,

Without thought, unlimited,
Its potency is ubiquitous in the ten directions.

Likewise the wisdom of the Buddha
Is in the minds of all beings,
Those who practice diligently
Will quickly attain the light of wisdom.

As the *nāga* has four jewels
Which engender all treasures,
Kept in a secret place,
Out of the sight of ordinary people.

Likewise the Buddha's four wisdoms
Engender all wisdom;
Other people cannot see them,
With the exemption of the great Bodhisattvas.

As the four jewels in the ocean
Can imbibe all water,
So that the ocean does not inundate,
And does not increase or decrease.

Likewise the wisdom of the Buddha
Ends unrestraint and abrogates spiritual attachments;
Vast, without bounds,
It can engender the Buddhas and Bodhisattvas.

From the lower regions up to the highest heaven,
The realms of desire, form, and formlessness,
All depends on space,
Whilst space does not differentiate.

The wisdom of the *śrāvakas,*
Pratyekabuddhas, and Bodhisattvas,
All depend on the Buddha's wisdom,
Whereas the Buddha's wisdom does not differentiate.

In the Himālayas there is a sovereign medicine
Called 'limitless roots'
Which can grow the roots, stems,
Leaves, and flowers of all trees.

Likewise the Buddha's wisdom
Is born from the seed of the Tathāgata;
Once it attains *bodhi,*
It further originates the Bodhisattva practices.

As someone who takes dry grass
And throws it into the fire on the end of a *kalpa;*
When even diamonds flare up,
The straw could do nothing but burn.

The *kalpas* and lands of the three times,
And the sentient beings therein—
That straw would sooner not burn,
Then the Buddha not know any of these.

There is a wind called 'devastation'
Which can destroy the great universe;
If not precluded by another wind,
It would destroy numberless worlds.

Likewise the wind of great wisdom
Obliterates the delusions of all Bodhisattvas,

Whilst another expedient wind
Causes them to abide at the stage of the Tathāgata.

As a great sūtra
As extensive as the great universe
It entirely contained within a singe particle of dust,
And likewise within all particles of dust.

There is a wise person who,
Clearly seeing with his pure eyes,
Breaks the particle of dust and takes out the sūtra,
Thus universally benefiting sentient beings.

Likewise the wisdom of the Buddha
Is in the minds of all sentient beings;
Enshrouded with false thoughts,
They are not aware of, nor know it.

The great kindness and compassion of all Buddhas
Induces them to renounce false thoughts,
So that the wisdom can manifest,
Benefiting all Bodhisattvas.

The Realm of the Tathāgata

"Children of the Buddha, how should Bodhisattva-mahāsattvas know the realm of the Tathāgata, Arhat, Perfectly Enlightened One?[119] Children of the Buddha, the Bodhisattva-mahāsattvas' knowing of the realm of all worlds by unhindered, unobstructed wisdom is the realm of the Tathāgata. Knowing the realm of the three times, the realm of all lands, the realm of all dharmas, the realm of all sentient beings, the undifferentiated realm of suchness, the unobstructed realm of the *dharmadhātu*, the limitless realm of the region of reality, the non-quantitative realm of space, the objectless realm is the realm of the Tathāgata. Children of the Buddha, as the realm of all worlds is boundless, so is the realm of the Tathāgata boundless; as the realm of the three times is boundless, so is the realm of the Tathāgata boundless, etc.; as the objectless realm is boundless, so is the realm of the Tathāgata boundless. As the objectless realm is non-existent everywhere, so is the realm of the Tathāgata non-existent everywhere.

"Children of the Buddha, Bodhisattva-mahāsattvas should know that the realm of mind is the realm of the Tathāgata. As the realm of mind is boundless, infinite, neither bound nor free, so is the realm of the Tathāgata boundless, infinite, neither bound nor free. Wherefore? Because it is by such and such thoughts and discernments that such and such boundless manifestations appear.

"Children of the Buddha, as the rain showered by the great *nāga* king according to his inclinations does not come from inside, nor does it come from outside, likewise the realm of the Tathāgata, in response to such infinite thoughts and discernments, has such infinite manifestations, none of which comes from any place in the ten directions. Children of the Buddha, as the water of the great ocean is all created by the mental power of the *nāga* king, in the same manner the ocean of all-encompassing wisdom of all the Buddhas, Tathāgatas, is created from the past great vows of the Tathāgata.

"Children of the Buddha, though the ocean of all-encompassing wisdom is boundless, infinite, inconceivable, and ineffable, I will now relate a few similes about it; you should listen attentively. Children of the Buddha, in this [continent] Jambudvīpa there are two thousand five hundred rivers flowing into the great ocean; in the western [continent] Godaniya there are five thousand rivers flowing into the great ocean; in the eastern [continent]

Purvavideha there are seven thousand five hundred rivers flowing into the great ocean; in the northern [continent] Uttarakuru there are ten thousand rivers flowing into the great ocean.[120] Children of the Buddha, these four continents altogether have twenty-five thousand rivers which uninterruptedly flow into the great ocean. What do you think, is that a lot of water?"

"Very much, indeed."

"Children of the Buddha, there is further the *nāga* king Ten Lights who rains twice that much water into the ocean; the *nāga* king Hundred Lights rains twice as much water as that into the ocean; the *nāga* king Extensive Adornments, the *nāga* king Mānasa, the *nāga* king Thunder, the *nāga* kings Nanda and Upananda, the *nāga* king Boundless Light, the *nāga* king Unremitting Rain, the *nāga* king Grand Triumph, the *nāga* king Great Enlivener—eighty billion such great *nāga* kings each rain into the ocean twice as much water as the previous one. The crown prince of *nāga* king Sāgara, called Jambu (Rose-apple) Pennant, further rains twice that much water into the great ocean. Children of the Buddha, the water from the palace of the *nāga* king Ten Lights flows into the great ocean, further twice that much; the water from the palace of the *nāga* king Hundred Lights flows into the ocean, further twice that much. The palaces of the *nāga* king Extensive Adornments, the *nāga* king Mānasa, the *nāga* king Thunder, the *nāga* kings Nanda and Upananda, the *nāga* king Boundless Light, the *nāga* king Unremitting Rain, the *nāga* king Grand Triumph, the *nāga* king Great Enlivener, and the rest of the eighty billion great *nāga* kings are each different, and the water from each of them flows into the great ocean, each of them twice as much as the previous. The water from the palace of Jambu Pennant, the crown prince of the *nāga* king Sāgara, flows into the great ocean, further twice as much as that. Children of the Buddha, the *nāga* king Sāgara further rains twice that much water into the great ocean; the water that emerges from the palace of the *nāga* king Sāgara and enters the ocean is further twice that much. That water is of a purplish color; it emerges occasionally, thus effecting the tide of the great ocean to be regular. Children of the Buddha, in such way is the water of the great ocean boundless, its treasures are boundless, its beings are boundless, and the earth it supports is also boundless. Children of the Buddha, what do you think: is the great ocean boundless?"

"It is truly boundless. It is beyond similitude."

"Children of the Buddha, the boundlessness of the great ocean, when compared with the boundlessness of the ocean of the Buddha's wisdom, does not reach a hundredth part of it, not a thousandth part, up to it does not reach even the minutest part of it. It is only for the sake of sentient beings that similes are told, whilst the realm of the Buddha transcends all similitude.

"Children of the Buddha, Bodhisattva-mahāsattvas should know that the ocean of the Tathāgata's wisdom is boundless because of the unrelenting cultivation of all Bodhisattva practices from the first arousal of the mind set on enlightenment (*bodhicitta*). They should know that its treasures are boundless, because all conditions leading to enlightenment and the seeds of the three treasures are indestructible. They should know that the sentient beings that dwell in it are boundless, because all those at the stage of learning and those beyond learning, *śrāvaka*s and *pratyekabuddha*s, obtain benefits from it. They should know that its dwelling ground is boundless, because it is the domicile of all Bodhisattvas, from the first stage of joy up to the final stage of non-obstruction. Children of the Buddha, Bodhisattva-mahāsattvas should, for the sake of entering boundless wisdom and benefiting sentient beings, thus know the realm of the Tathāgata, Arhat, Perfectly Enlightened One."

At that time, wishing to once more enunciate the meaning of

this, Samantabhadra Bodhisattva-mahāsattva uttered the following verses:

As the realm of mind is boundless,
So is the realm of all Buddhas;
As the realm of mind is created from mentation,
So should the realm of the Buddha be perceived.

As the nāga without leaving his abode,
By his awesome mental power pours profuse rain;
Though the rainwater has no place of coming and going,
According to the nāga's mind it spreads everywhere.

Likewise the ten-powered Muni
Comes from nowhere and goes nowhere;
If one has a pure mind, then he manifests a body:
Extensive as the *dharmadhātu*, it enters a hair pore.

As the treasures of the ocean are boundless,
So too are its beings and land;
The nature of its water is uniform, without variance,
Those living in it each obtain benefit.

The ocean of the Tathāgata's wisdom is also like this—
Everything in it is boundless;
Those at the stage of learning and those beyond learning,
All obtain benefit in it.

The Activity of the Tathāgata

"Children of the Buddha, how should Bodhisattva-mahāsattvas know the activity of the Tathāgata, Arhat, Perfectly Enlightened One? Children of the Buddha, Bodhisattva-mahāsattvas should know that unobstructed activity is the activity of the Tathāgata; they should know that the activity of suchness (*tathatā*) is the activity of the Tathāgata. Children of the Buddha, as suchness is unborn in the past, unmoving in the future, and non-arising in the present, likewise the activity of the Tathāgata is unborn, unmoving, and non-arising. Children of the Buddha, as the *dharmadhātu* is neither measurable nor measureless, because it is formless, so is the activity of the Tathāgata neither measurable nor measureless, because it is formless.

"Children of the Buddha, as a bird that flies through space for a hundred years: the places it passes and those it does not pass will both be impossible to measure. Wherefore? Because the realm of space is unlimited. The activity of the Tathāgata is also thus: if there was a person who spent numberless *kalpas* explicating its different aspects, what has been said and what has not been said would both be impossible to measure. Wherefore? Because the activity of the Tathāgata is unlimited.

"Children of the Buddha, the Tathāgata, Arhat, Perfectly Enlightened One, abides in unobstructed activity without having abode, but he can still reveal his activity to all sentient beings, so that when they see it they transcend all paths of encumbrance. Children of the Buddha, when Garuḍa,[121] the king of birds, flies across the sky, it soars in circles, watching for the palaces of the *nāgas*. Arousing its mighty strength, it stirs up the water of the ocean with its wings, causing it to open up. Then, knowing which male and female *nāgas* are about to end their life, it seizes them away.

"The Tathāgata, Arhat, Perfectly Enlightened One, Garuḍa king of birds, is also thus: abiding in unobstructed activity, with his pure Buddha-eye he observes all sentient beings in all places through the *dharmadhātu*. For those whose planted wholesome roots are already mature, the Tathāgata arouses his mighty ten powers, and with the two wings of calmness (*śamatha*) and insight (*vipaśyanā*) he stirs up the great waters of desire of the ocean of birth and death, opening them up so as to seize those beings and place them within Buddhadharma, effecting them to cease all false thoughts and erroneous differentiations, and to securely dwell in the non-discriminatory, unobstructed activity of the Tathāgata.

"Children of the Buddha, as the sun and the moon traverse the sky alone, without a companion, thus benefiting sentient beings, but have no idea about where they come from and where they go, likewise all the Buddhas, Tathāgatas, their nature fundamentally quiescent, without discrimination, appear to travel across all *dharmadhātus.* Because they wish to benefit all sentient beings, they engage in all Buddha-activities without repose, without giving rise to such false discriminations as, 'I am coming from there, and am going there.' Children of the Buddha, Bodhisattva-mahāsattvas, by such boundless means, such boundless nature and phenomena, should perceive the actions performed by the Tathāgata, Arhat, Perfectly Enlightened One."

Then Samantabhadra Bodhisattva, wishing to once more enunciate the meaning of this, uttered the following verses:

As suchness has no creation and destruction,
Has no locus, and cannot be seen,
So does the activity of the Supreme Benefactor
Go beyond the three realms, impossible to measure.

The *dharmadhātu* is not a realm, nor is not not a realm,
It neither has measure nor is measureless;
Likewise the activity of the one with great merit
Neither has measure nor is measureless, because it is
incorporeal.

As when a bird flies for a billion years,
The space in front and behind it is commensurate;
When the activity of the Tathāgata is narrated for
many *kalpas,*
The expressed and the unexpressed are both immeasurable.

Garuḍa from the sky watches the great ocean,
Opens the water, and seizes male and female *nāgas;*
The Ten-powered culls those with wholesome roots,
Causing them to leave the ocean of existence and abrogate
their illusions.

As the sun and the moon traverse the sky,
Shining on everything without discrimination,
The World-Honored moves throughout the *dharmadhātu,*
Edifying sentient beings without a stirring thought.

The Accomplishment of Perfect Enlightenment of the Tathāgata

"Children of the Buddha, how should all Bodhisattva-mahāsattvas know the accomplishment of perfect enlightenment (*saṁbodhi*) of the Tathāgata, Arhat, Perfectly Enlightened One?[122] Children of the Buddha, Bodhisattva-mahāsattvas should know that the accomplishment of perfect enlightenment of the Tathāgata has no perception of any object, is equanimous toward [all] dharmas, has no doubts, is non-dual, formless, inactive; [it] has no stoppage, no measure, no limitations. Forsaking the two extremes, it abides in the Middle Way and transcends all words and letters. It knows the minds and mental activities of all sentient beings, their faculties, natures, predilections, afflictions, and defiling habits. To sum up, within a single thought it knows all dharmas of the three times.

"Children of the Buddha, as because the great ocean can

reflect the physical appearances of all sentient beings in the four continents, it is commonly spoken of as the great ocean. Likewise the *bodhi* of all Buddhas universally manifests in the minds, thoughts, faculties, natures, and predilections of all sentient beings, without manifesting anything. Hence it is called the *bodhi* of all Buddhas.

"Children of the Buddha, the *bodhi* of all Buddhas all writings cannot describe, all voices cannot reach, all languages cannot explicate. It is only expediently explained in response to necessity.

"Children of the Buddha, when the Tathāgatas, Arhats, Perfectly Enlightened Ones, accomplish perfect enlightenment, they obtain bodies of the same magnitude as all sentient beings; they obtain bodies of the same magnitude as all dharmas; they obtain bodies of the same magnitude as all lands; they obtain bodies of the same magnitude as all three times; they obtain bodies of the same magnitude as all Buddhas; they obtain bodies of the same magnitude as all speeches; they obtain bodies of the same magnitude as suchness; they obtain bodies of the same magnitude as the *dharmadhātu*; they obtain bodies of the same magnitude as the realm of space; they obtain bodies of the same magnitude as the realm of non-obstruction; they obtain bodies of the same magnitude as all vows; they obtain bodies of the same magnitude as all practices; they obtain bodies of the same magnitude as the quiescent realm of Nirvāṇa. Children of the Buddha, as are the bodies they obtain, so are their speeches and minds. They obtain such boundless, innumerable pure three wheels [of body, speech, and mind].

"Children of the Buddha, when the Tathāgatas, Arhats, Perfectly Enlightened Ones, accomplish perfect enlightenment, they perceive that within their own body all sentient beings accomplish perfect enlightenment, until they perceive that all sentient beings enter Nirvāṇa. All have the same nature, which is absence of nature. Absence of what kind of nature? It is absence of the nature of form, absence of the nature of depletion, absence of the nature of birth, absence of the nature of destruction, absence of the nature of self, absence of the nature of non-self, absence of the nature of sentient being, absence of the nature of non-sentient being, absence of the nature of *bodhi*, absence of the nature of the *dharmadhātu*, absence of the nature of space, and also absence of the nature of accomplishment of perfect enlightenment. Because of knowing that all dharmas have no nature, they attain all-encompassing wisdom and with great compassion continue to deliver sentient beings.

"Children of the Buddha, like space that never increases or diminishes whether all worlds are created or destroyed. Wherefore? Because space is uncreated. The *bodhi* of all Buddhas is also thus: whether they accomplish perfect enlightenment or do not accomplish perfect enlightenment, it does not increase or diminish. Wherefore? Because *bodhi* neither has form nor is formless, is neither one nor many.

"Children of the Buddha, suppose there is a person who can create minds as numerous as the sands of the Ganges river, and each of those minds can further produce Buddhas as numerous as the sands of the Ganges river, all without form, appearance, or marks, continuing to do so without respite for as many *kalpas* as the sands of the Ganges river. Children of the Buddha, what do you think: how many Tathāgatas would be produced by the minds created by that person?"

Sublime Virtue of Nature Origination of the Tathāgata Bodhisattva replied, "As I understand the meaning of what has been said, creation and non-creation are equal, without distinction. How can one ask how many there would be?"

Samantabhadra Bodhisattva said: "Excellent! Excellent, son of the Buddha, [it is] just as you said. Even if all sentient beings instantaneously accomplish perfect enlightenment, that would in no way be different from nobody accomplishing perfect enlightenment. Wherefore? Because *bodhi* is formless. Since it is formless, it does not increase or diminish. Children of the Buddha, Bodhisattva-mahāsattvas should thus know the accomplishment of perfect enlightenment—equal to *bodhi*, its only sign is signlessness.

"When the Tathāgatas accomplish perfect enlightenment by means of the single sign, they enter the *samādhi* of the wisdom of adroit awareness. After they have entered [into that *samādhi*], in a single vast body that accomplishes perfect enlightenment, [each of them] manifests bodies equal in number to all sentient beings dwelling in that body. As it is with one vast body that accomplishes perfect enlightenment, so it is with all vast bodies that accomplish perfect enlightenment. Children of the Buddha, the Tathāgatas have such boundless ways of accomplishment of perfect enlightenment. Therefore, it should be known that all bodies manifested by the Tathāgata are boundless. Because they are boundless, it is said that the body of the Tathāgata is a boundless realm, equal to the realm of sentient beings.

"Children of the Buddha, Bodhisattva-mahāsattvas should know that within a single pore of the body of the Tathāgata there are Buddha-bodies equal in number to all sentient beings. Wherefore? Because the body of the Tathāgata's accomplishment of perfect enlightenment ultimately has no creation and destruction. As a single pore pervades the *dharmadhātu*, so it is with all pores.[123] It should be known that there is not an infinitesimal place where the Buddha's body is not present.[124] Wherefore? Because there is no place where the accomplishment of perfect enlightenment of the Tathāgata does not reach. In accordance with ability, in accordance with power, on the lion seat under the *bodhi* tree at the site of enlightenment, with various bodies [the Tathāgata] accomplishes perfect enlightenment.

"Children of the Buddha, Bodhisattva-mahāsattvas should know that within each thought of their own minds there is always the Buddha's accomplishment of perfect enlightenment. Wherefore? It is not outside of this mind that all the Buddhas, Tathāgatas, accomplish perfect enlightenment. As it is with one's own mind, so it is with the minds of all sentient beings—within each of them there is the Tathāgatas accomplishment of perfect enlightenment. Vast and universal, there is no place where it is not present. Without alienation or effacement, without respite, entering the Dharma-teaching of inconceivable means. Children of the Buddha, Bodhisattva-mahāsattvas should thus know the accomplishment of perfect enlightenment of the Tathāgata."

Then Samantabhadra Bodhisattva, wishing to once more enunciate the meaning of this, uttered the following verses:

The Perfectly Enlightened comprehends all dharmas
Are non-dual, transcend duality, are equal;
Their self-nature is pure as space,
Without discriminating self and not-self.

As the ocean reflects the bodies of sentient beings,
Which is the reason for its being called great ocean,
Bodhi reflects all mental activity,
Therefore it is called perfect enlightenment.

As worlds have creation and decay,
While space does not increase or diminish,
Though all the Buddhas manifest in the world,
The only sign of *bodhi* is its signlessness.

As when a person creates minds that produce Buddhas,
The natures of creation and non-creation are not different;
Even if all sentient beings accomplish bodhi,
With accomplishment or without, there is no increase or diminishment.

The Buddha has a *samādhi* called 'adroit awareness';
When he enters this *samādhi* under the bodhi tree,
He emits boundless lights as numerous as beings,
Enlightening the multitudes like lotuses opening.

As the thoughts and desires
Of the beings of all lands and times,
Bodies of such number appear—
Therefore perfect enlightenment is called boundless.

The Turning of the Dharma-wheel

"Children of the Buddha, how should Bodhisattva-mahāsattvas know the turning of the Dharma-wheel (*dharma-cakra*) of the Tathāgata, Arhat, Perfectly Enlightened One? Children of the Buddha, Bodhisattva-mahāsattvas should know it as this: the Tathāgata turns the Dharma-wheel by his independent mental power, without arising or turning, because he knows that all dharmas never arise; he turns the Dharma-wheel by the three turnings,[125] obliterating what needs to be obliterated, because he knows that all dharmas leave the [two] extreme views (*antar-grāha-dṛṣti*);[126] he turns the Dharma-wheel leaving the limit and the limitlessness of desire, because he enters the limit of all dharmas which is like space; he turns the Dharma-wheel without speech, because he knows that all dharmas are ineffable; he turns the Dharma-wheel ultimately quiescent, because he knows that all dharmas are of the nature of Nirvāṇa; he turns the Dharma-wheel by the means of all writings and languages, because there is no place where the voice of the Tathāgata does not reach; he turns the Dharma-wheel knowing that the voice is like an echo, because he realizes the real nature of all dharmas; he turns the Dharma-wheel generating all sounds from a single sound, because ultimately there is no master; he turns the

Dharma-wheel without default and conclusion, because of not attaching to inside and outside.

"Children of the Buddha, as all writings and languages cannot be completely told until the end of time, so it is with the Buddha's turning of the Dharma-wheel—all words are established to reveal it, without recess, without ever consummating it. Children of the Buddha, the Dharma-wheel of the Tathāgata enters all speeches and writings, without abiding anywhere. As writing enters all events, all languages, all reckonings, all mundane and supramundane locations, without abiding anywhere, so does the voice of the Tathāgata enter all places, all sentient beings, all dharmas, all actions, and all retributions, without abiding anywhere. The various speeches of all sentient beings are not asunder from the Dharma-wheel of the Tathāgata. Whence? Because the reality of words and sounds is itself the Dharma-wheel. Children of the Buddha, Bodhisattva-mahāsattvas should thus know the turning of the Dharma-wheel of the Tathāgata.

"Further, children of the Buddha, if Bodhisattva-mahā-sattvas wish to know the Dharma-wheel turned by the Tathāgata, they ought to know the place of origin of the Dharma-wheel of the Tathāgata. What is the place of origin of the Dharma-wheel of the Tathāgata? Children of the Buddha, in accord with the infinite differences among the mental activities and predilections of all sentient beings, the Tathāgata engenders many voices and turns the Dharma-wheel. Children of the Buddha, the Tathāgata, Arhat, Perfectly Enlightened One, has a *samādhi* called 'ultimate non-obstruction and fearlessness.' After he has entered this *samādhi*, with each mouth of each body of accomplishment of perfect enlightenment, he produces voices as numerous as all sentient beings. Each of these voices contains numerous distinct voices, turning the Dharma-wheel, and thus causing all sentient beings to rejoice. It should be known that those who thus know the turning of the Dharma-wheel comply with all Buddhadharmas. Those who do not thus know it do not comply. Children of the Buddha, all Bodhisattva-mahāsattvas should thus know the turning of the Dharma-wheel of the Buddha, because it universally enters boundless realms of sentient beings."

Then Samantabhadra Bodhisattva-mahāsattva, wishing to once more enunciate the meaning of this, uttered the following verses:

The Dharma-wheel of the Tathāgata does not turn,
It does not arise and is unobtainable in the three times;
As writing is never exhausted,
So is the Dharma-wheel of the Ten-powered.

As words enter all without reaching,
Likewise the Dharma-wheel of the Perfectly Enlightened
Enters all words and sounds without entering anything,
Able to cause all sentient beings to rejoice.

The Buddha has a *samādhi* called 'ultimate';
After entering this *samādhi* he expounds the Dharma,
Limitless as all sentient beings might be,
His voice enlightens them all.

With each voice he also enunciates
Boundless distinct words and sounds;
Sovereign in the world, not discriminating,
Enabling all to hear according to their wishes.

Letters do not emanate from inside or outside,
Are not destroyed and do not accumulate;
Yet for the sake of beings the Dharma-wheel is turned—
Such freedom is most preternatural.

The Parinirvāṇa of the Tathāgata

"Children of the Buddha, how should Bodhisattva-mahāsattvas know the *parinirvāṇa* of the Tathāgata? Children of the Buddha, if Bodhisattva-mahāsattvas wish to know the great Nirvāṇa of the Tathāgata, they must realize the fundamental self-nature. As is the Nirvāṇā of suchness, so is the Nirvāṇa of the Tathāgata; as is the Nirvāṇā of the limit of reality, so is the Nirvāṇa of the Tathāgata; as is the Nirvāṇa of the *dharmadhātu,* so is the Nirvāṇa of the Tathāgata; as is the Nirvāṇa of space, so is the Nirvāṇa of the Tathāgata; as is the Nirvāṇa of the Dharma-nature, so is the Nirvāṇa of the Tathāgata; as is the Nirvāṇa of the limit of desirelessness, so is the Nirvāṇa of the Tathāgata; as is the Nirvāṇa of the limit of formlessness, so is the Nirvāṇa of the Tathāgata; as is the Nirvāṇa of the limit of self-nature, so is the Nirvāṇa of the Tathāgata; as is the Nirvāṇa of the limit of the nature of all dharmas, so is the Nirvāṇa of the Tathāgata; as is the Nirvāṇa of the limit of suchness, so is the Nirvāṇa of the Tathāgata. Wherefore? Because Nirvāṇa is unborn and unoriginated. If a dharma is unborn and unoriginated, then it has no extinction.

"Children of the Buddha, the Tathāgata does not relate the final Nirvāṇa of all Tathāgatas to the Bodhisattvas, nor does he reveal it to them. Whence? Because he wants to enable them to perceive all Tathāgatas evermore present in front of them, to perceive within a single thought all past and future Buddhas, replete with their distinguishing marks, as if they have truly appeared, without creating any conception of duality or nonduality. Wherefore? Because Bodhisattva-mahāsattvas permanently relinquish all conceptual attachments.

"Children of the Buddha, all the Buddhas, Tathāgatas, for the sake of gladdening sentient beings manifest in the world; because they wish sentient beings to experience yearning they manifest Nirvāṇa. But in reality the Tathāgatas do not manifest in the world, nor do they [enter] Nirvāṇa. Wherefore? The Tathāgatas eternally abide in the pure *dharmadhātu,* manifesting Nirvāṇa in response to the mentalities of sentient beings.

"Children of the Buddha, like when the sun appears, it shines on the whole world, so that its reflection is visible in all receptacles filled with clean water. Though [the sun] is ubiquitous, it has no coming and going. If a receptacle is broken, then the reflection in it disappears. Children of the Buddha, what do you think: is it the sun's fault that its reflection has disappeared?"

"No, it is solely due to the destruction of the receptacle. It is not the sun's fault."

"Children of the Buddha, likewise the sun of wisdom of the Tathāgata manifests throughout the *dharmadhātu,* without past and future. The Buddha manifests in the clean mind-receptacles of all sentient beings. If the mind-receptacle is always clean, then one always perceives the body of the Buddha; if the mind is corrupted and the receptacle is broken, then one is unable to perceive [the Buddha].

"Children of the Buddha, if there are sentient beings that should be saved with Nirvāṇa, the Tathāgata manifests Nirvāṇa for them, but in reality the Tathāgata has no birth, no death, and no extinction (Nirvāṇa).

"Children of the Buddha, it is like the fire element which in all worlds performs the work of fire. If the fire was extinguished at some place, do you think that the fires in all the worlds will be extinguished?"

"No."

"Children of the Buddha, likewise the Tathāgata, Arhat, Perfectly Enlightened One, in all worlds performs the Buddha-activity; if in one world he has accomplished what could have been done, he enters Nirvāṇa. But that does not mean that all the Buddhas, Tathāgatas, in all other worlds enter extinction. Children of the Buddha, Bodhisattva-mahāsattvas should thus know the great Nirvāṇa of the Tathāgata, Arhat, Perfectly Enlightened One.

"Children of the Buddha, like a thaumaturge apt at thaumaturgy, who by the power of his thaumaturgy manifests illusory bodies in the towns and villages of all lands in the great universe, sustained for the duration of a *kalpa* by his thaumaturgic power, while at other sites after his thaumaturgy has ended the illusory bodies disappear. Children of the Buddha, what do you think: when the illusory bodies of the great thaumaturge disappear at one location, do they also disappear everywhere else?"

"No."

"Children of the Buddha, likewise the Tathāgata, Arhat, Perfectly Enlightened One, knowing well the various thaumaturgies of boundless wisdom and means, manifests his body throughout all *dharmadhātus*, permanently sustained to the end of time. If in one place, in response to beings' mentalities, he accomplishes his work, he then enters Nirvāṇa. But because he has manifested entry into Nirvāṇa in one place, how can it be considered that he has become extinct everywhere? Children of the Buddha, Bodhisattva-mahāsattvas should thus know the great Nirvāṇa of the Tathāgata, Arhat, Perfectly Enlightened One.

"Further, children of the Buddha, when the Tathāgata, Arhat, Perfectly Enlightened One, manifests Nirvāṇa, he enters the unmoving *samādhi*. After he has entered this *samādhi* from each body he emanates infinite hundreds of thousands of billions of great lights; from each light further emerge *asaṅkhyas* of lotuses, each of them having untold sublime precious stamens. On each stamen there is a lion seat, and atop of each lion seat there is a Tathāgata sitting cross-legged. The number of bodies of those Buddhas is precisely the same as the number of sentient beings. All of them are imbued with sublime adornments of merit, produced by the power of their original vows. If there are sentient beings whose wholesome roots are mature, when they see those Buddha bodies they are edified, while those Buddha bodies ultimately abide to the end of time, saving all sentient beings as appropriate without missing an opportunity.

"Children of the Buddha, the body of the Tathāgata is without locus, is neither true nor false—it only manifests by the power of the original vows of all Buddhas and the sentient beings' aptitude to be saved. Bodhisattva-mahāsattvas should thus know the great *parinirvāṇa* of the Tathāgata, Arhat, Perfectly Enlightened One.

"Children of the Buddha, the Tathāgata dwells in the boundless, unobstructed, ultimate *dharmadhātu*, in the realm of space, in the Dharma-nature of suchness, without creation or destruction, and in the region of reality. For the sake of all sentient beings he always manifests, supported by the original vows, without respite, not leaving all sentient beings, all lands, all dharmas."

At that time Samantabhadra Bodhisattva-mahāsattva, wishing to once more enunciate the meaning of this, uttered the following verses:

As the sun emits light which irradiates the *dharmadhātu,*
When a receptacle is broken the water spills out and the
  reflection vanishes;
So is the sun of peerless wisdom:
When beings have no faith they perceive Nirvāṇa.

As fire performs the work of fire in the world,
It goes out in one town at some time;
The supreme among men pervades the *dharmadhātu,*
Manifesting passing away where his edifying work is
  completed.

As a thaumaturge manifests bodies in all lands,
That wither when his artistry lapses;

Likewise when the Tathāgata has completed his edifying
work,
In other lands the Buddha is always seen.

The Buddha has a *samādhi* called 'unmoving'
That he enters after he has edified sentient beings;
Within an instant his body issues boundless light,
From the light emerge lotuses with Buddhas on them.

The Buddha's bodies are numberless, equal to the
dharmadhātu,
Perceivable by sentient beings with blessings;
Each of these numberless bodies
Is complete with life span and adornments.

Like the unborn nature is the Buddha's appearance,
Like the undying nature is the Buddha's Nirvāṇa;
All words and similes cease,
All objectives accomplished, without equal.

The Wholesome Roots Planted by Seeing, Hearing, and Associating with the Tathāgata

"Children of the Buddha, how should Bodhisattva-mahāsattvas know the wholesome roots planted by seeing, hearing, and associating with the Tathāgata? Children of the Buddha, Bodhisattva-mahāsattvas should know that all wholesome roots planted by seeing, hearing, and associating with the Tathāgata are not false, because they produce the infinite wisdom of enlightenment; because they forsake all obstructions; because they explicitly reach the ultimate; because they are free from deception; because [they cause] all vows to be fulfilled; because they do not abrogate conditioned activity; because they comply with the wisdom of the unconditioned; because they produce the wisdom of all Buddhas; because they exhaust the future; because they consummate all superior practices; because they arrive at the stage of effortless wisdom.

"Children of the Buddha, like a man who swallows a little diamond, in the end he will be incapable to digest it, and it will have to pass through his body to get outside. Wherefore? Because diamonds do not coexist with the various impurities within the physical body. Likewise, small wholesome roots planted with the Tathāgata will have to pass through the body of all conditioned formations and afflictions, and reach the abode of unconditioned final wisdom. Wherefore? These small wholesome roots do not coexist with conditioned formations and afflictions.

"Children of the Buddha, if on a pile of dry grass as big as Sumeru [mountain] someone throws even the smallest spark of fire, [the whole pile] will inevitably be completely consumed. Wherefore? Because the fire has the capacity to ignite. Likewise small wholesome roots planted with the Tathāgata will inevitably consume all afflictions and finally [capacitate one to] attain Nirvāṇa without residue (*anupadhiśeṣa*). Wherefore? Because the nature of these small wholesome roots is ultimate.

"Children of the Buddha, in the Himālayas there is a sovereign healing tree called 'good to see.' If anyone sees it, his eyes are purified; if anyone hears it, his ears are purified; if anyone smells it, his nose is purified; if anyone tastes it, his tongue is purified; if anyone touches it, his body is purified; if there are sentient beings who take its soil, that will also benefit them by removing their illnesses. Children of the Buddha, likewise the Tathāgata, Arhat, Perfectly Enlightened One, unsurpassed sovereign healer, can bestow all benefits: if sentient beings see his physical body, their eyes are purified; if they hear the name of the Tathāgata, their ears are purified; if they smell the perfume of discipline (*śīla*) of the Tathāgata, their noses are purified; if they taste the flavor of the Dharma of the Tathāgata, their tongues are purified, and they obtain broad and long tongues and understanding of the ways of speech;[127] if they come in contact with the light of the Tathāgata, their bodies are purified, and they ultimately procure the unsurpassed *dharmakāya*; if they think of the Tathāgata, they attain the purity of the *samādhi* of reflection on the Buddha; if any sentient beings make offerings to the ground where the Tathāgata has passed, to stūpas and temples, they too consummate their wholesome roots, obliterate the plague of all afflictions, and obtain the happiness of the sages.

"Children of the Buddha, I will now tell you: if there are sentient beings who see or hear the Buddha, [but because of being] bound by their karmic obstructions they do not give rise to faith and joy, they will also without failure plant wholesome roots, until they finally enter Nirvāṇa. Children of the Buddha, Bodhisattva-mahāsattvas should thus know that all wholesome roots planted by seeing, hearing, and associating with the Tathāgata are asunder from all unwholesome (*akuśala*) dharmas, and replete with wholesome (*kuśala*) dharmas.

"Children of the Buddha, the Tathāgata with all similes explains many things, but there is no simile that can explain this principle. Wherefore? Because the ways of mind and knowledge are cut off, and it is inconceivable. All Buddhas and Bodhisattvas relate similes only for the purpose of causing sentient beings to rejoice in accord with their mentalities; [however,] that is not conclusive.

"Children of the Buddha, this Dharma-teaching is called the arcane abode of the Tathāgata; it is called that which cannot be known by [anyone] in all worlds; it is called entering the seal of the Tathāgata; it is called opening the great gate of wisdom; it is called revealing the seed-nature of the Tathāgata; it is called perfecting all Bodhisattvas; it is called that which cannot be destroyed in all worlds; it is called completely complying with the realm of the Tathāgata; it is called able to purify the realms of all sentient beings; it is called explicating the ultimate inconceivable Dharma of the fundamental true nature of the Tathāgata.[128]

"Children of the Buddha, the Tathāgata does not disclose this Dharma-teaching to any other sentient beings except to the Bodhisattvas disposed toward the Great Vehicle (Mahāyāna); he discloses it only to those Bodhisattvas who have mounted the Inconceivable Vehicle. This Dharma-teaching does not come in the hands of any sentient beings except all Bodhisattva-mahāsattvas.

"Children of the Buddha, like the seven treasures possessed by the wheel-turning universal monarch (*cakravartī-rāja*) that symbolize his status as a universal monarch. These treasures do not come into the hands of any sentient being, except the crown prince born by his first wife who has fully accomplished the attributes of a universal monarch. If the wheel-turning universal monarch does not have such a son replete with numerous virtues, then seven days after the monarch's passing away the treasures will all evanesce.

"Children of the Buddha, the treasure of this sūtra is also thus: it does not come into the hands of any other sentient beings except the true children of the Tathāgata, the Dharma monarch, who are born in the family of the Buddhas and plant all wholesome roots specific to the Buddhas. Children of the Buddha, if there were no such true children of the Buddha, then this Dharma-teaching will disappear before long. Wherefore? All those of the two vehicles do not hear this sūtra, let alone receive and uphold it, read, recite, and transcribe it, comprehend and explicate it. This can only be done by all Bodhisattvas. Therefore, when Bodhisattva-mahāsattvas hear this Dharma-teaching they greatly rejoice; with a reverential attitude they respectfully accept it. Wherefore? Because

Bodhisattva-mahāsattvas who trust and rejoice in this sūtra will quickly attain *anuttara-samyak-saṃbodhi.*

"Children of the Buddha, if a Bodhisattva for boundless billions of *kalpas* practices the six *pāramitās*[129] and cultivates the various conditions leading to enlightenment (*bodhipākṣika dharma*), but has not heard this Dharma-teaching of the inconceivable noble virtues of the Tathāgata, or has heard it but does not believe in it, does not understand it, does not comply with it, and does not enter into it, he is not to be called a true Bodhisattva, because he cannot be born in the family of the Tathāgata. If he hears this teaching of the boundless, inconceivable, unobstructed, unimpeded wisdom of the Tathāgata, having heard it believes in it, understands it, complies with it, becomes enlightened and enters into it, it should be known that this person is born in the family of the Tathāgata, that he complies with the realm of all the Tathāgatas, securely abides in the realm of perfect wisdom (*sarvākarajñatā*),[130] has consummated all dharmas pertaining to the Bodhisattvas, has forsaken all mundane dharmas, manifests the activity of all Tathāgatas, penetrates the essential-nature (*dharmatā*) of all Bodhisattvas, has no doubts about the Buddha's freedom, abides in the Dharma without a teacher, and profoundly enters the unobstructed realm of the Tathāgatas.

"Children of the Buddha, after Bodhisattva-mahāsattvas have heard this Dharma, then they can with the wisdom of universality (*samatā-jñāna*) know infinite dharmas; then they can with straightforward mind forsake all discriminations; then they can by their supreme aspiration perceive all Buddhas; then they can by the power of their resolve enter the equanimous realm of space; then they can by the means of free thought travel across the limitless *dharmadhātu*; then they can by the power of wisdom consummate all merit; then they can by natural wisdom forsake all worldly defilements; then they can by the means of *bodhicitta* enter all principles in the ten directions; then they can by their supreme contemplation know that all Buddhas of the three times are of the same essential nature; then they can by the wisdom of dedication of wholesome roots universally enter the such-like Dharma, enter without entering, without grasping a single dharma, evermore contemplating all dharmas by the means of one dharma. Children of the Buddha, Bodhisattva-mahāsattvas accomplish such merit; applying a little effort they attain natural wisdom without a teacher."

Then Samantabhadra Bodhisattva-mahāsattva, wishing to once more enunciate the meaning of this, uttered the following verses:

The merit obtained by seeing, hearing,
And making offering to all the Buddhas is immeasurable;
Ultimately inexhaustible in terms of the conditioned,
It obliterates afflictions and forsakes suffering.

Like a man who swallows a small diamond,
In the end it will come out undigested;
The merit of making offerings to the Ten-powered
Obliterates delusions and ensures attainment of diamond wisdom.

As a pile of straw big as Sumeru
Will be consumed by a small spark of fire,
The little merit from making offerings to all Buddhas
Will certainly efface the afflictions and lead to Nirvāṇa.

In the Himālayas there is a medicine called 'good to see'
The seeing, hearing, smelling, or touching of which cures all illnesses;
Those who see or hear the Ten-powered
Obtain supreme merit and realize the Buddha's wisdom.

Epilogue

At that time, because of the preternatural power of the Buddha, and because of the way things are, in each of the ten directions there were untold hundreds of thousands of billions of worlds that quaked in six different ways, viz.: rising in the east, sagging in the west; rising in the west, sagging in the east; rising in the south, sagging in the north; rising in the north, sagging in the south; rising on the edges, sagging in the middle; rising in the middle, sagging on the edges. They [also] moved in eighteen different ways, viz.: moving, moving everywhere, equally moving everywhere, rising, rising everywhere, equally rising everywhere, bouncing, bouncing everywhere, equally bouncing everywhere, quaking, quaking everywhere, equally quaking everywhere, roaring, roaring everywhere, equally roaring everywhere, striking, striking everywhere, equally striking everywhere.

There rained clouds of all flowers, clouds of all canopies, clouds of banners, clouds of pennants, clouds of incenses, clouds of wreaths, clouds of scents, clouds of ornaments, clouds of brilliant *maṇi* jewels, clouds of Bodhisattvas reciting eulogies, clouds of different bodies of untold Bodhisattvas, each of these surpassing those of all heavens. It [also] rained clouds of accomplishment of perfect enlightenment, clouds purifying inconceivable worlds; it rained clouds of sounds of the speeches of the Tathāgatas, filling the limitless *dharmadhātu.* As the preternatural power of the Tathāgata was thus manifested in this world, bringing great joy to all Bodhisattvas, so it was throughout all worlds in the ten directions.

Then, in each of the ten directions, past worlds as numerous as the particles of dust of eighty untold hundreds of thousands of billions of Buddha-lands, there were Tathāgatas [as numerous as] the particles of dust of eighty untold hundreds of thousands of billions of Buddha-lands, all of them called

Samantabhadra, who manifested in front [of the assembly].

They said, "Excellent, son of the Buddha! You are able to receive the awesome power of the Buddha and expound the inconceivable Dharma of the manifestation of the Tathāgata in conformity with the Dharma-nature. Child of the Buddha, all of us, Buddhas of the same name as numerous as the particles of dust of eighty untold hundreds of thousands of billions of Buddha-lands, explicate this Dharma. As we explicate it, so do all the Buddhas in the worlds of the ten directions. Child of the Buddha, now in this assembly Bodhisattva-mahāsattvas numerous as the particles of dust of a hundred thousand Buddha-lands attained the *samādhi* of the preternatural powers of all Bodhisattvas. On them we confer the prophecy that within a single lifetime they will attain *anuttara-samyak-saṃbodhi*. Sentient beings numerous as the particles of dust of a Buddha-land awoke the mind set on *anuttara-samyak-saṃbodhi*; on them we also confer the prophecy that in future, after *kalpa*s numerous as the particles of dust of untold Buddha-lands, they will all become Buddhas with the same name—Preternatural Realm of the Buddha. In order to enable all Bodhisattvas in the future to hear this Dharma, we will all protect and preserve it together. As is with the sentient beings saved in this world, so it is with the sentient beings saved in all hundreds of thousands of billions, countless, infinite, and so on, until untold, ineffable, equal to the *dharmadhātu* and space, worlds of the ten directions."

At that time, because of the awesome preternatural power of all Buddhas in the ten directions, because of the power of the original vows of Vairocana, because of the way things are, because of the power of the wholesome roots, because the Tathāgatas' actuation of wisdom does not go beyond a [single] thought, because the Tathāgatas respond to circumstances without missing an opportunity, because they always enlighten all Bodhisattvas, because past actions are not lost or destroyed, because they effect the extensive practices of Samantabhadra, because they manifest the freedom of the all-encompassing wisdom, in the ten directions past worlds as numerous as the particles of dust of ten untold hundreds of thousands of billions of Buddha-lands, there were Bodhisattvas as numerous as the particles of dust of ten untold hundreds of thousands of billions of Buddha-lands, who came here, filling all *dharma-dhātus* in the ten directions, manifesting the extensive adornments of Bodhisattvas, issuing networks of great lights, quaking all worlds in the ten directions, obliterating all mansions of Māra, extinguishing the sufferings of all evil paths, manifesting the noble virtues of all Tathāgatas, singing eulogies of the boundless unique merits of the Tathāgatas, raining all kinds of rain, manifesting infinite distinct bodies, receiving all boundless Buddhadharmas.

By the preternatural power of the Buddha, each of them said, "Excellent, son of the Buddha! You can explicate this indestructible Dharma of the Buddha. Son of the Buddha, the name of all of us is Samantabhadra; we have all come here from the sites of Universal Pennant Freedom Tathāgatas in the Universal Light worlds. In all those places this Dharma is also expounded with identical words and sentences, identical meanings, identical explanations, identical peremptoriness, without augmentation or deduction. We have, by the preternatural powers of the Buddhas, and because of having attained the Dharma of the Tathāgatas, come here to testify to you. As is with us coming here, it is the same in the lands of all worlds in the ten directions, equal to space, throughout the *dharmadhātu*."

At that time, Samantabhadra Bodhisattva, supported by the preternatural power of the Buddhas, surveyed the great assembly of Bodhisattvas, and wishing to once more enunciate the vast noble virtue of the manifestation of the Tathāgata; the indelibility of the correct Dharma of the Tathāgata; how the boundless wholesome roots are not empty; the necessity to consummate all supreme dharmas for the Buddhas to appear in the world; the dexterous observation of the minds of all sentient beings; the teaching of the Dharma in response to needs without missing an opportunity; the creation of the boundless Dharma-lights of all Bodhisattvas; the adornment of freedom of all Buddhas; how all Tathāgatas have one body, without distinction, engendered by their original supreme practices, he uttered the following verses:

The acts of all Tathāgatas
All similes in the world do not reach;
For the sake of enabling beings to attain enlightenment,
Non-similes are taken as similes in order to demonstrate them.

Such subtle, arcane Dharma,
Is difficult to hear in a billion kalpas;
Those with vigor, wisdom, and restraint,
Are able to hear this recondite principle.

Those who delight when they hear this Dharma
Have already made offerings to boundless Buddhas;
Protected by the power of the Buddhas,
Humans and gods praise them and make offerings to them.

This is the supreme treasure which transcends the world,
This can save all living beings,
This can engender the pure Path—
You should upkeep it without slackening!

Notes

1. Yo kho dhammam passati so maṃ passati; yo maṃ passati so dhammam passati. Dhammaṃ hi passanto maṃ passati; maṃ passanto dhammam passati. *Saṃyutta-Nikāya*, vol. 3 (London: Pāli Text Society, 1975), p. 120. The English translation is that by Bhikkhu Ñāṇamoli from his *The Life of the Buddha* (Kandy, Sri Lanka: Buddhist Publication Society, 1978), p. 198.

2. This kind of reasoning is especially often found in the texts of the Ch'an school. For example, Ta-chu Hui-hai (n.d.), one of the best known disciples of Ma-tsu (709–788), is recorded as saying, "Mind is Buddha, so there is no need to seek the Buddha by Buddha. Mind is the Dharma, so there is no need to seek the Dharma by Dharma. The Buddha and the Dharma are not two, and when they are in harmonious union, then there is the Sangha. These are the three treasures of one essence." *Ching-te ch'uan-teng lu, chüan* 28, Ta-chu's entry.

3. The *Avataṃsaka Sūtra*, T vol. 10, p. 64c.

4. This is not meant to imply that all Buddhist doctrines, or even most of them, are mutually compatible. However, there is certainly much more common ground among the teachings of the various schools than often acknowledged. When properly understood and used, the various teachings are more often than not mutually complementary.

5. T vol. 10, p. 438a.

6. HYCS, T vol. 35, p. 959b.

7. The essence, characteristics, and function paradigm is found in the *Treatise on the Awakening of Faith* (*Ta-sheng*

ch'i-hsin lun, T 1666, vol. 32). This treatise exerted enormous influence on the development of Chinese Buddhism; its influence is especially observable in the works of the Hua-yen masters. "Essence" refers to suchness, the ultimate reality, or the way things are; "characteristics" refers to the myriad virtues of that essence, such as wisdom, compassion, etc.; "function" is the activity that results when the essence responds to conditions.

8. *Li* and *shih* are philosophical concepts with long history in Chinese thought that predate the introduction of Buddhism to China. The principle (sometimes translated as "noumenon") and phenomena paradigm is often employed in the texts of the Hua-yen school, and familiarity with these two concepts is vital for understanding Hua-yen thought. Simply put, *li* can be interpreted as the absolute, or the ultimate truth, and *shih* as phenomena, or phenomenal appearances. We will come across this pair of concepts again in this Introduction, and we hope their meaning will become clearer within the contexts in which they are used.

9. See HYCS, T vol. 35, p. 959b.

10. T vol. 10, p. 81c. Cf. Thomas Cleary, *The Flower Ornament Scripture*, vol. 1 (Boston & London: Shambhala, 1984), p. 373.

11. T vol. 10, p. 82a. Cf. Cleary, vol. 1, p. 374.

12. See under "The Characteristics of the Manifestation of the Tathāgata" in this volume's translation.

13. T vol. 10, p. 72b. Cf. Cleary, vol. 1, p. 331.

14. For an explanation of *dharmadhātu* see "Related Doctrines" later in the Introduction.

15. See, for example, Francis H. Cook, *Hua-yen Buddhism: The*

Jewel Net of Indra (University Park: The Pennsylvania State University, 1977), p. 21. The connection with Khotan has been underscored by Kamekawa Kyōshin. See his *Hua-yen hsüeh*, translated into Chinese by Shih Yin-hai (Hsin-chu: Wu-liang shou ch'u-pan she, 1988), pp.36–38.

16. T vol. 10, pp. 445a–446b. It roughly corresponds to chapter 7 of Śikṣānanda's translation of the *Avataṃsaka Sūtra*. It also includes parts of its ninth chapter.

17. T vol. 10, pp. 446b–450c. It includes chapters 9, 11, and 15 of Śikṣānanda's translation.

18. T vol. 10, pp. 851c–876a.

19. More detailed discussion on this subject can be found in Liu Ming-Wood, "The Teaching of Fa-tsang: An Examination of Buddhist Metaphysics" (Ph.D. diss., University of California, Los Angeles, 1979), pp. 34–36.

20. Biography in *Kao seng chuan*, T vol. 50, p. 334b–335c.

21. T vol. 9, pp. 395a–788b.

22. Biography in *Sung kao seng chuan*, T vol. 50, pp. 718c–719a.

23. T vol. 10, pp. 1b–444c.

24. T vol. 10, pp. 661a–848b. It corresponds to the Sanskrit *Gaṇḍavyūha Sūtra*.

25. It is interesting to note that two of the translations of the *Avataṃsaka*, the most representative of the Mahāyāna sūtras, were done by monks associated with the Sarvāstivāda school, the most flourishing of the so-called Hīnayāna schools. And this is not an isolated case; we find the same situation with other translations of Mahāyāna works into Chinese. This certainly says something about the degree of

sectarianism—or rather the lack of it—in Indian Buddhism, and perhaps has something to teach the present-day followers of the Buddha.

26. Liu, p. 56, n. 54.

27. The identification of the *Avataṃsaka Sūtra* with the Hua-yen school is natural considering the influence the first exerted on the second, as well as the amount of exegetical material on the *Avataṃsaka* composed by the Hua-yen masters. However, it is also important to distinguish between the two. As a philosophical system Hua-yen Buddhism is perhaps more indebted to the philosophical systems of Indian Mahāyāna Buddhism—most noticeably the Tathāgatagarbha and Yogācāra—than to the *Avataṃsaka,* though there is no doubt that the *Avataṃsaka* served as the main source of inspiration and final point of reference to the founders of this tradition. While the writings of the Hua-yen school are rightly used as the main texts for interpreting the *Avataṃsaka,* it can also be pointed out that they are only one way of interpreting this profound scripture. The essential teaching of the *Avataṃsaka* itself defies any attempt to capture it in any doctrinal system, no matter how profound. That is of course fully understood and accounted for in the Hua-yen system.

28. Chinese text in *Ching-te ch'uan-teng lu, chüan* 30. For an English translation see Thomas Cleary, *Timeless Spring: A Soto Zen Anthology* (Tokyo: John Weatherhill, Inc., 1980), pp. 36–37.

29. T vol. 10, pp. 592c–617b.

30. Biography in *Kao seng chuan,* T vol. 50, pp. 326c–327a.

31. E. Zurcher, *The Buddhist Conquest of China* (Leiden: E. J. Brill, 1972), p. 65–70.

32. T vol. 9, pp. 611b–631b.

33. T vol. 35, pp. 79b–82a. The page references in this and the subsequent four notes refer to the sections of those works that contain the commentaries on the "Manifestation" chapter.

34. T vol. 35, pp. 405a–418b.

35. HTC vol. 5, p. 260b–273d. This commentary on the new translation of the *Avataṃsaka* was started by Fa-tsang toward the end of his life, but was left unfinished at his death, later to be completed by Hui-yüan.

36. T vol. 35, pp. 871c-887b. Ch'eng-kuan also wrote a sub-commentary on this commentary, entitled *Hua-yen ching sui-shu yen-i ch'ao* in 90 *chüan* (T 1736, vol. 36). There is an excellent Taiwanese edition that contains the text of the sūtra, the commentary, and the sub-commentary: *Hua-yen ching shu ch'ao* (Taipei: Hua-yen lien-shih), in 10 vols.

37. T vol. 36, pp. 938a–941c.

38. HYCS, T vol. 35, p. 871c.

39. T vol. 45, p. 514a–b. Tradition has it that this treatise was recorded by Chih-yen on the basis of oral instructions given by his teacher Fa-shun (557–640), also known as Tu-shun, who is regarded as the first patriarch of the Hua-yen school. The passage quoted was brought to my attention by Robert M. Gimello's thesis, "Chih-yen (602–668) and the Foundations of Hua-yen Buddhism" (Ph.D. diss., Columbia University, 1976), p. 425. This thesis is the best work on the doctrinal and social influences that led to the formation of the Hua-yen school in English that I am aware of, as well as the only work that gives fuller treatment to the life and thought of Chih-yen, in some ways

the actual founder of the Hua-yen school.

40. T vol. 10, pp. 1c–2a. Cf. Cleary, vol. 1, p. 56.

41. *Hua-yen kuan-mo i-chi*, T vol. 45, p. 657c. Quoted by Liu, p. 89.

42. T vol. 36, p. 938a.

43. T vol. 35, p. 405a.

44. This simplified version of the structure of the *Avataṃsaka* and the place of the Manifestation" chapter in it is in general agreement with Fa-tsang's fivefold classification of the contents of the *Avataṃsaka*. When speaking in terms of the five rounds of cause and fruit, another classification scheme developed by Fa-tsang, the "Manifestation" chapter, together with the proceeding chapter, the "Samantabhadra's Practice" chapter, belongs to the third round of cause and fruit. Fa-tsang calls this round of cause and fruit "equal cause and fruit." According to him, the "Samantabhadra's Practice" chapter describes the "equal perfect cause," Samantabhadra's practice being the cause for the attainment of Buddhahood, while the "Manifestation" chapter describes the "equal full fruit"—the full fruition of Buddhahood. See *Hua-yen ching t'an-hsüan chi*, T vol. 35, p. 120b. Also see Kamekawa, pp. 47–48, and Liu, pp. 110–111.

45. This is the well-known definition of the "Tathāgata" from the *Diamond Sūtra*.

46. An alternative translation could read: "ancient attainment and new Buddha," and "new attainment and ancient Buddha."

47. HYCS, T vol. 35, pp. 871c–872a.

48. Liu gives the Sanskrit name of this Bodhisattva as Tathāgataniyataguna. Liu, p. 100.

49. HYCS, T vol. 35, p. 872b.

50. Ibid.

51. *The Aṅguttara-Nikāya*, vol.1 (Oxford: Pāli Text Society, 1961), p. 10. The English translation is from F. L. Woodward, *The Book of Gradual Sayings*, vol. 1 (London: Pāli Text Society, 1932), p. 8.

52. T vol. 48, p. 404b–c. Also see Jeffrey Lyle Broughton, "Kuei-feng Tsung-mi: The Convergence of the Ch'an and the Teachings" (Ph.D. diss. Columbia University, 1975), pp. 188–189. A similar passage appears in Tsung-mi's *Yüan-jen lun* (*Treatise on the Origin of Man*), T vol. 45, p. 710a. For its English translation, see Gregory, "What Happened to the Perfect Teaching? Another Look at Hua-yen Buddhist Hermeneutics," in Donald S. Lopez, ed., *Buddhist Hermeneutics* (Honolulu: University of Hawaii Press, 1988), p. 214.

53. See the last simile in "The Mind of the Tathāgata" in this volume's translation. I have adapted parts of the translation from Gregory, "What Happened to the 'Perfect Teaching'?" pp. 214–215.

54 See, for example, about the role this passage played in Chinul's second major awakening in Robert E. Buswell, *The Korean Approach to Zen: The Collected Works of Chinul* (Honolulu: University of Hawaii Press, 1983), pp. 24–25.

55. *Ta-sheng ch'i-hsin lun i-chi*, T vol. 44, p. 243b–c. Also see Gregory, *Tsung-mi and the Sinification of Buddhism* (Princeton: Princeton University Press, 1991), p. 157.

56. Here Tsung-mi uses the unusual *chen-chieh*, which I have

translated as the "realm of reality," which he identifies as the *dharmadhātu* of suchness (*chen-ju fa-chieh*).

57. The Dharma-lakṣaṇa (*fa-hsiang*) approach is most often associated with Hsüan-tsang's (ca. 596–664) brand of Yogācāra. It is often contrasted with the teaching of the Dharma-nature (*fa-hsing*), which is the teaching of the Hua-yen school championed by Tsung-mi.

58. Meaning the Hua-yen teaching of Dharma-nature.

59. HTC vol. 7, p. 399c. See Peter N. Gregory, "What Happened to the Perfect Teaching?" p. 222.

60. *Wang-chin huan-yüan kuan*, T vol. 45, p. 639b.

61. Here Fa-tsang uses the well-known statement from the *Vimalakīrti Sūtra* as a scriptural support for his explication: "All dharmas are established with non-abiding as a basis."

62. See Gregory, *Tsung-mi*, p. 242.

63. See under "The Accomplishment of Perfect Enlightenment of the Tathāgata" in this volume's translation.

64. T vol. 45, p. 678b. I have adapted the translation from Gimello, p. 491. See also Gimello's comments on this passage.

65. T vol. 45, p. 678c.

66. *Hua-yen ching sou-hsüan chi*, T vol. 35, p. 87c. Gimello, p. 458.

67. *Hua-yen ching t'an-hsüan chi*, T vol. 35, p. 440b.

68. Ibid.

69. *Hua-yen ching t'an-hsüan chi*, T vol. 35, p. 440b; Liu, pp. 391–394. See also Gregory, *Tsung Mi*, p.8. For Ch'eng-kuan's definition of *dharmadhātu*, see T vol. 35, pp.

907c–908a; and for Li T'ung-hsüan's see T vol. 36, p. 943b–c.

70. See Gregory, *Tsung-mi*, p. 8.

71. The fourth *dharmadhātu* in Ch'eng-kuan's theory of four *dharmadhātus*. The other three are the *dharmadhātu* of phenomena (*shih fa-chieh*), the *dharmadhātu* of principle (*li fa-chieh*), and the *dharmadhātu* of non-obstruction between principle and phenomena (*li-shih wu-ai fa-chieh*).

72. In his *Wu-chiao chang* Fa-tsang mentions a passage from the "Entering the *Dharmadhātu*" chapter as a scriptural support, or inspiration, for his contention that the teaching of the *Avataṃsaka* represents the "perfect teaching." See T vol. 45, p. 481b. For an English translation of the relevant passage, see Cook, "Fa-tsang's Treatise on the Five Doctrines: An Annotated Translation" (Ph.D. diss., University of Wisconsin, 1970), pp. 173–174.

73. See Gregory, *Tsung-mi*, pp. 155–156.

74. In Cook's translation, the six characteristics are: universality, particularity, identity, difference, integration, and disintegration. See Francis H. Cook, *Hua-yen Buddhism*, p. 77.

75. *Wu-chiao chang*, T vol. 45, p. 507c. Also Cook, *Hua-yen Buddhism*, p. 77.

76. See Gregory, *Tsung-mi*, p. 242.

77. See the third simile under "The Mind of the Tathāgata" in this volume's translation.

78. See "The Accomplishment of Perfect Enlightenment of the Tathāgata" section in this volume's translation.

79. Ibid.

80. *Hsin hua-yen ching lun*, T vol. 36, p. 941a–c. Cf. Buswell, pp. 204–205.

81. In the Śikṣānanda's translation of the *Avataṃsaka Sūtra*, from chapter 27, the "Ten Samādhis" chapter, to the end of chapter 37, the "Manifestation of the Tathāgata" chapter, the exposition of the sūtra is taking place in the Universal Light hall, in the seventh assembly of the sūtra (of which there are nine altogether).

82. According to Fa-tsang the emanation of light from the white curl between the Buddha's eyebrows symbolizes the correct realization of the ten stages, that is, the full realization of the Bodhisattva Path. *Hua-yen ching wen-i kang-mu*, T vol. 35, p. 499c.

In his commentary Ch'eng-kuan explains that the space between the eyebrows symbolizes enlightenment, "because it leaves the two extremes of existence and non-existence." Or, according to the Taishō version, it symbolizes "the realization of the Middle Way." It also symbolizes "the way of non-abiding, because it leaves the two extremes of the real and the provisional." The white curl symbolizes that the nature of that which is to be revealed—the realm of Buddhahood—because it is undefiled, and can illustrate the source of all teachings. See HYCS, T vol. 35, p. 872a.

83. Fa-tsang relates four purposes for the Buddha's emanation of lights: (1) to reveal the Dharma, (2) to astound the audience and cause them to engender faith, (3) to disclose suffering with the intention of saving sentient beings form it, and (4) to summon and gather the multitudes from afar. *Hua-yen ching wen-i kang-mu*, T vol. 35, p. 499c. Also see Liu, pp. 115–116.

84. For an explanation of *dharmadhātu* see "Related Doctines"

in the Introduction.

85. For an explanation of the name of this Bodhisattva see the "Content Summary" in the Introduction. The entry of the light emanated from the Buddha into the Bodhisattva symbolizes the empowerment of the Bodhisattva by the Buddha. Its entry into the crown of the Bodhisattva's head symbolizes that the sublime wisdom of Buddhahood can be revealed in its ultimate scope.

86. The light coming from the mouth exemplifies the unhindered transmission of the Teaching. The name of the light signifies unobstructed eloquence, and absence of intimidation, both from the audience and from the profundity of the Truth that is to be expounded.

87. Samantabhadra Bodhisattva, together with Mañjuśrī, is the principal Bodhisattva of the *Avataṃsaka Sūtra*. Samantabhadra Bodhisattva symbolizes the cultivation and perfection of the myriad practices that constitute the Bodhisattva Path. For further references on Samantabhadra Bodhisattva, see the Introduction.

88. Instead of "manifestation," here, as well as throughout the text, Buddhabhadra's translation has "nature origination." The same phrase also appears in the title of Buddhabhadra's translation of this chapter—"Nature Origination of Precious King Tathāgata" chapter.

89. Literal translation of the term would be something like "three-thousand-great-thousand universe." It stands for a great universe, or chiliocosm, which is the realm of one Buddha. Such a universe consists of one thousand middle universes, each of which consists of one thousand small universes, while each small universe comprises one thousand worlds. Thus, the great universe consists of

one billion worlds.

90. According to ancient Indian cosmology, the circle of wind (*vāyu-māṇḍala)* is a whirlwind of air that supports the world. It is situated below the circles of water and metal on which the earth rests. The wind-circle itself rests on space.

91. Instead of "perceive" Buddhabhadra's translation has "know and perceive." The same expression is used in the rest of the questions that open every new section of the text.

92. Buddhabhadra's translation has "one act" (*i hsing*) instead of "one phenomenon" (*i shih*).

93. The conditions, or practices, that are favorable to, or lead to, enlightenment. They are thirty-seven in number, and are: the four applications of mindfulness (*smṛtyupasthāna*), the four correct efforts (*samyakpradhāṇa*), the four steps toward mystical power (*ṛddhipāda*), the five spiritual faculties (*indriyāni*), the five powers (*bala*), the seven factors of enlightenment (*bodhyaṅga*), and the eight-fold noble path (*aṣṭāṅga-mārga*).

94. Vairocana Buddha, the Buddha of the Flower Treasury World, represents the absolute and eternal aspect of universal Buddhahood. In terms of the three bodies of a Buddha he symbolizes the *dharmakāya*, the essential body which is identical in all the Buddhas. For further references on Vairocana, see the Introduction.

95. The first absorption, or meditation, is the first of the four states of mental focus and undivided concentration during which there is absence of sensory activity. The standard description of the first absorption found in the scriptures, especially in the Pāli canon, is: "Quite secluded from sense desires, secluded from unprofitable things he enters upon and dwells in the first jhana (absorption), which is

accompanied by applied and sustained thought with happiness and bliss born of seclusion." Quoted by Buddhaghosa in his *Visuddhimagga* from the *Vibhaṅga* 245. The English translation is from Bhikkhu Ñāṇamoli, *The Path of Purification* (Colombo: R. Semage, 1956), p. 144.

96. The Brahmā heavens, or Brahmāloka, here refer to the first three of the eighteen heavens in the realm of form. They are also known as the heavens of the first absorption, because those who attain the first absorption are reborn there.

97. The classical description of the second absorption is: "With the stilling of applied and sustained thought he enters upon and dwells in the second jhana (absorption), which has internal confidence and singleness of mind without applied thought, without sustained thought, with happiness and bliss born of concentration." *Vibhaṅga* 245; Ñāṇamoli, pp. 161–162.

98. The third, and highest of the three heavens of the second absorption, also known as the heaven of universal light, so-called because its inhabitants are said to communicate by lights instead of words.

99. The classical description of the third absorption is: "With the fading away of happiness as well he dwells in equanimity, and mindful and fully aware he feels bliss with his body, he enters upon and dwells in the third jhana, on account of which the Noble Ones announce: 'He dwells in bliss who has equanimity and is mindful.'" *Vibhaṅga* 245; Ñāṇamoli, p. 165.

100. The third of the three heavens of the third absorption in the realm of form.

101. The classical description of the fourth absorption is: "With the abandoning of pleasure and pain and with the previous disappearance of joy and grief he enters upon

and dwells in the fourth jhana, which has neither pain nor pleasure and has purity of mindfulness due to equanimity." *Vibhaṅga* 245; Ñāṇamoli, p. 171.

102. The third of the eight heavens of the third absorption, also known as the heaven where those of exalted deeds are born.

103. The ruler of the Brahmalokas, or Brahmā heavens, in the realm of form.

104. This is the sixth, and highest, of the six heavens in the realm of desire, which float above the top of Sumeru mountain. It is said that the pleasures of the other five heavens of the realm of desire can be enjoyed in this heaven.

105. The fifth of the six heavens in the realm of desire, where the inhabitants produce their object of pleasure by themselves.

106. The fourth heaven of the realm of desire, where the future Buddhas reside before their final rebirth.

107. The second of the six heavens in the realm of desire. It is the heaven of the thirty-three gods who live atop Sumeru mountain. It is ruled by Indra, who resides in its center.

108. This is the northern of the four continents that surround Sumeru mountain. It is said to be square in shape, and is described as being superior to the other three continents because of the long life span of its inhabitants and the ease with which they obtain food without physical effort.

109. While in the *Avataṃsaka* the *sāgaramudrā samādhi* is listed only as one of the many *samādhi*s mentioned in the text, the Hua-yen tradition singled out this particular *samādhi* as representing the ultimate scope and depth of the Buddha's awareness. This *samādhi* plays a prominent role

in the writings of the Hua-yen school—especially in Fa-tsang's writings—where it is taken as a symbol for the Buddha's enlightenment. In his treatise the *Contemplation of Practicing the Profound Purport of Avataṃsaka which Extinguishes Falsehood and Returns to the Source* Fa-tsang explains this *samādhi* in the following way: "Ocean Seal is the original enlightenment of true suchness. When all falsehood is extinguished the mind becomes clear and still, so that the myriad images equally appear in it. It is like the great ocean on whose surface waves appear because of wind; when the wind ceases, the water of the ocean becomes clear and still, so that there are no images that are not reflected in it." T vol. 45, p. 637b.

110. Ch'eng-kuan notes that this passage has been the subject of a lot of discussion in the past. He mentions some of the opinions upheld by different masters. He divides them into two groups: (1) The first group (represented by some Yogācārins), which can further be sub-divided into two groups, conceives of the mind, mental states, and consciousness of the Buddha as existent. Some from this group maintain that there are two kinds of mental activity: pure and impure. At the stage of Buddhahood there is no impure mind or mental activity, but there is pure mind and mental activity. Others maintain that it is said that the mind of the Buddha is unobtainable because it is free from discriminating thoughts. But the non-discriminatory wisdom of the Buddha, which is limitless, is not apart from mind. (2) The second group maintains that at the stage of Buddhahood there is no mind, nor any mental activity. That is why the text says they "are unobtainable." There is only wisdom, here identified with the wisdom of suchness, which is the reason why the text says "because wisdom is boundless, one can know the mind of the Tathāgata."

Ch'eng-kuan points out that both of these views are partial and deficient. The first two explanations (which conceive of the Buddha's mind as existent) do not accord with the statement "are unobtainable." The second explanation (which says that at the stage of Buddhahood there is no mind or mental activity) does not accord with the statement "know the mind of the Tathāgata." Concerning the second view, Ch'eng-kuan questions: if there is only the wisdom of suchness, then how can there be wisdom outside of the mind?

Further down, Ch'eng-kuan explains:

> As to the phrase 'are unobtainable,' because the mind's meaning is abstruse, words cannot reach it. The manifestation of the profound is thus concealed. As to the statement that only by wisdom can one know the mind of the Tathāgata, that allows for the place of mental conditions, thus revealing the profound... Why is it abstruse? If we say it is existent, it is identical with suchness, devoid of characteristics. If we say it is non-existent, its profound wonder is not exhausted... If we say it is one, it contains [everything], there being nothing outside of it. If we say it is many, it has a single taste and is impossible to divide... When the mouth wants to talk about it, it is left without words. When the mind wants to think about it, all thoughts cease.

In the final analysis, says Ch'eng-kuan, the mind of the Buddha cannot be known or described solely in terms of existence or non-existence, purity or impurity, sameness or difference, etc. Conversely, because the fruit of Buddhahood is ineffable, the mind of the Buddha can be conceived of (by someone endowed with wisdom who does not cling to words) as both existent and non-existent, as both principle and phenomenon, one and many. That being so, there is perfect fusion and non-obstruction. HYCS, T vol. 35, p. 878a–b.

111. An ancient Indian measure of distance described as the day's march of a royal army; it is equal to four *krosas*, which is about nine English miles, or thirty Chinese *li*. Soothill and Hodous, *A Dictionary of Chinese Buddhist Terms,* p. 197b.

112. These are the mountains that encircle the earth. They form the periphery of the world.

113. The higher of the two circles of mountains that enclose the world. They form the outer periphery of the world.

114. Ch'eng-kuan explains these two statements in the following way: "Therefore, to know that the Buddha's wisdom is everywhere [means that] there is no sentient being that is not possessed of original enlightenment, which does not differ from the essence of Buddhahood." Ch'eng-kuan then explains the three meanings of the statement that all sentient beings have the Buddha's wisdom: (1) First, the statement clarifies that there is not a single sentient being that does not have the Buddha's wisdom. That which does not have Buddha-nature is not a sentient being. Here Ch'eng-kuan seems to equate *tathāgatajñāna* with *buddhadhātu*. Indeed, quoting the *Nirvāṇa Sūtra*, further down Ch'eng-kuan writes "Buddha-nature is called wisdom." In his sub-commentary he also quotes the famous passage from the *Nirvāṇa Sūtra* to illustrate the meaning of his explanation. In that passage it is stated that, with the exception of (things like) walls, tiles, and stones, everything else has Buddha-nature. That

which does not have Buddha-nature is not a sentient being. Everything that has a mind is bound to become a Buddha. (2) Even while at the causal ground of bondage, sentient beings already fully possess the fruit (of Buddhahood) which is beyond bondage. (3) The wisdom of fruition in the causal state is identical with the wisdom of fruition of all other Buddhas. According to the school of the perfect teaching, the essence of the cause and fruit of self and others are not different. This teaching, concludes Ch'eng-kuan, is unique to the Hua-yen school. HYCS, T vol. 35, p. 880a.

115. The all-encompassing wisdom is the wisdom that comprehends all dharmas, viz., their emptiness. The spontaneous wisdom is the Buddha's wisdom which is obtained spontaneously, without application of effort and without the guidance of a teacher. Ch'eng-kuan identifies it with the "holy wisdom of self-enlightenment" (*tzu-chueh sheng-chih*), so-called because it is attained by self-enlightenment without the help of a teacher. That is Vairocana's "wisdom of the essential nature of the *dharmadhātu*." The unobstructed wisdom is explained by Ch'eng-kuan as the "[realization of the] non-duality of acquired [enlightenment] and original [enlightenment]." (HYCS, T vol. 35, p. 880b) Acquired and original enlightenment are terms that appear in the *Awakening of Faith*. In his sub-commentary Ch'eng-kuan explains their non-duality in two ways: (1) Since sentient beings originally possess the Buddha's wisdom, the original enlightenment does not obstruct the acquired enlightenment. The realization of this is called "unobstructed wisdom." (2) When all hindrances are removed and enlightenment is realized, then the two obstructions—of defilements and to the knowable—cease to operate.

116. A universe which consists of a million worlds. A thousand such universes form the great universe, which is one Buddha-world, consisting of a billion worlds.

117. A universe with a thousand worlds. Thousand such universes form a medium universe.

118. For the importance of this passage see the Introduction.

119. The realm of the Buddha can be understood both (1) in terms of the fruition of Buddhahood which has the consummation of the ten Bodhisattva stages as its cause, and (2) as the object of the Buddha's unobstructed awareness—the realm of reality, or the way the universe truly is. The realm of the Buddha is often alluded to or elaborated on throughout the *Avataṃsaka Sūtra.* One section in the sūtra where the realm of the Buddha is explained in more detail is the last part of the "Bodhisattvas Ask for Elucidation" chapter. There all Bodhisattvas in the assembly ask Mañjuśrī Bodhisattva about the realm of the Buddha. Mañjuśrī answers their questions in ten verses. Each of the verses addresses one facet of the realm of the Buddha, as defined in the questions.

1. The realm of the Tathāgata in terms of its profundity and vastness:

   The Tathāgata's profound realm
   Is as extensive as space;
   All sentient beings enter into it,
   Without really entering anything.

According to Ch'eng-kuan the statement that all beings enter the realm of the Buddha without really entering has three meanings: (1) Since all beings are already the *tathāgatagarbha,* there is nothing really to enter. All they have to do is to awaken from their ignorance, which is why, in this case, the meaning of entering is that of "entry [through] realization." (2) From the perspective of the principle (i.e., ultimate reality), the relationship between sentient beings and the realm of the Buddha is neither that of identity nor of difference, which is why the text says "enter...without entering." (3) From the perspective of the "realm of mind," because the mind is at first ignorant of the realm of reality, we can speak of "entry." But if there is something really entered, then the dichotomy of wisdom and its object is not transcended, in which case it is impossible to speak of (real) entering. Because there is nothing that is really entered, it is called suchness. Thus, explains Ch'eng-kuan, the realm of the Buddha is vast and profound, transcending speech and thought.

2. The causes of the realm of the Tathāgata:

   The Tathāgata's profound realm's
   Supreme sublime causes
   Even if continuously expounded for a hundred
      million *kalpa*s
   Could not be fully exhausted.

3. The liberation of the realm of the Tathāgata:

   In accord with their minds and wisdom,
   Guiding and benefiting all,
   Thus it liberates sentient beings—
   The realm of all Buddhas!

4. Entry into the realm of the Tathāgata:

   Of all lands in the world,
   Able to enter them all,
   The body of wisdom is without form,
   And is not an object of perception by others.

5. The wisdom of the realm of the Tathāgata:

   The wisdom of all Buddhas is sovereign,

Unobstructed by anything in the three times;
The realm of such wisdom
Is equal, like space.

6. The Dharma of the realm of the Tathāgata:
The *dharmadhātu* and the realms of beings
Are ultimately not different;
Fully realizing all of them,
That is the realm of the Tathāgata.

7. The explanations of the realm of the Tathāgata:
In all worlds
All sounds that are therein,
The Buddha's wisdom comprehends them all,
Without any discrimination.

8. The awareness of the realm of the Tathāgata:
Not an object of perception,
And not of the realm of mind,
Its nature fundamentally pure,
It edifies all sentient beings.

9. The realization of the realm of the Tathāgata:
Not an action, not a defilement,
Without thing, without abode,
Without reflection, devoid of all activity,
It equally acts throughout the world.

As Ch'eng-kuan's commentary nicely points out: "Because it is devoid of function, its function fills the *dharmadhātu*; because it is devoid of reflection, there is nothing that it does not know; because it is without locus, there is no place where it is not. Thus, the last sentence says, 'It equally acts throughout the world.' That is the arcane store of the three virtues (of liberation, wisdom, and the *dharmakāya*)—the realm of the Buddha!"

10. The manifestation of the realm of the
    Tathāgata:
  The minds of all beings
  Throughout the three times,
  The Tathāgata, within a single thought,
  Clearly comprehends them all.

T vol. 10. p. 69a–b. Also cf. Cleary, vol. 1, pp. 310–311. For Ch'eng-kuan's commentary see HYCS, T vol. 35, p.612a–c.

120. According to ancient Indian cosmology, these are the four inhabited continents of every world. They are situated to the south, east, west, and north of the Sumeru mountain, which is in the center of the world.

121. Garuḍa is the mythical king of the birds which has golden wings. It symbolizes the Buddha.

122. Instead of "accomplishment of perfect enlightenment" Buddhabhadra's translation has "*bodhi.*"

123. This sentence can also be translated: "As it is with one pore, so it is with all pores throughout the *dharmadhātu.*" My translation follows Ch'eng-kuan's comments on this passage.

124. An alternative translation could read: "There is not an infinitesimal place where there is no body of a Buddha."

125. The three turnings of the Dharma-wheel, which could be distinguished in the Buddha's teaching when he expounded the four noble truths in the Deer Park, are: (1) The turning of indication, which indicates the truth of suffering, its origins, its cessation, and the Path; (2) the turning of exhortation to practice, in which he exhorts to understand suffering, to obliterate its causes, to realize its cessation, and practice the Path; (3) the turning of realization, which consists of the awareness that suffering has been

understood, its origins have been obliterated, its cessation has been realized, and the Path has been practiced.

126. These are the two extreme views that attach to the beliefs in nihilism and eternalism, or permanence.

127. Broad and long tongue is one of the thirty-two distinguishing marks of a Buddha.

128. Commenting on the last part of this paragraph, Ch'engkuan says that the unchanging nature that responds to conditions is the origin of all Buddhas. Because nature and characteristics do not obstruct each other, and because cause and fruit are perfectly interfused, it is said to be "inconceivable." It is "ultimate" because there is nothing that can surpass it. HYCS, T vol. 35, p. 886a–b.

129. The six *pāramitās* are: (1) generosity (*dāna*), (2) precepts (*śīla*), (3) patience (*kṣānti*), (4) energetic application (*vīrya*), (5) meditation (*dhyāna*), and (6) wisdom (*prajñā*).

130. This is one of the three wisdoms. It is the Buddha-wisdom that perfectly knows all phenomena in all their aspects and relationships, in the past, present, and future. This wisdom is unique to the Buddhas.

Glossary

anuttara-samyak-saṁbodhi: "unexcelled perfect enlightenment," the enlightenment, or *bodhi*, of a Buddha, which is the most consummate universal awareness, as well as the wisdom and knowledge of that comprehensive awareness.

Arhat: one who is free from afflictions and further rebirths, the highest stage of holiness in the *śrāvaka* vehicle; one of the epithets of a Buddha.

asaṅkhya: innumerable, countless.

asura: fighting gods, or demons.

bodhi: enlightenment, awakening; the realization of reality.

bodhicitta: the mind that aspires toward perfect enlightenment.

Bodhisattva: a being who is fully dedicated to the goal of complete enlightenment and universal liberation.

Brahmā: the highest god who rules the world.

Buddha: someone who has achieved complete enlightenment; the reality itself.

Buddhadharma: see *Dharma*.

Buddha-nature: the pure, unalloyed, luminous essence of the mind of all sentient beings, which symbolizes their potential to achieve Buddhahood.

chüan: a division of a book, used in classical Chinese works.

dhāraṇī: mystical invocation, spell, mantra.

Dharma: ultimate truth, the reality as perceived by a Buddha; the teachings that lead to personal realization of that reality; (when lowercased) elemental entities that make up phenomena; any phenomena—thing, event, concept, idea, etc.

dharmadhātu: the "Dharma-element" or the "realm of reality," the sublime recondite essence of things; the universe in its totality.

Dharma-eye: the eye of truth that perceives reality.

dharmakāya: Dharma-body, the absolute aspect of reality, the essence of Buddhahood which is identical in all Buddhas; one of the three bodies of a Buddha.

Dharma-nature: *dharmatā*, the absolute nature underlying all phenomena; Reality. Often used as a synonym for Nirvāṇa, Buddha-nature, suchness, etc.

gandharva: Indra's heavenly musicians.

Jambudvīpa: the southern continent, where humans reside.

kalpa: eon, age, immensely long period of time.

karma: any physical, verbal, or mental activity that produces a result; the universal law that every action brings consequences that are largely determined by the nature of that action.

kinnara: mythical beings, one of the eight classes of heavenly musicians.

Mahāyāna: the "Great Vehicle" that reveals the complete liberation of all sentient beings; Bodhisattva Path of universal salvation.

Māra: demon; personification of forces, both internal and external, that obscure the true nature and lead one away from the Buddha's Path.

Middle Way: the way between the two extremes of existence

and nothingness that reveals the reality of all things.

mind-ground: the pivotal basis of the mind from which all things spring.

Muni: sage, saint.

nāga: serpent-gods who bring clouds and rain.

Nirvāṇa: complete liberation characterized by absence of delusion and permanent bliss, perfect quiescence.

One Vehicle: see *vehicle.*

pāramitā: "perfection," it stands both for the crossing over the sea of birth and death, and the means, or practices which effectuate that.

parinirvāṇa: the state of perfect quiescence entered by a Buddha upon the dissolution of his physical body.

pratyekabuddha: self-enlightened sage.

samādhi: state of mental imperturbability and clarity, meditative absorption.

saṃsāra: the cycle of birth and death.

saṅgha: the community of Buddhist monks (*bhikṣu*) and nuns (*bhikṣuṇi*); the community of Buddhist saints who have attained the different stages of enlightenment.

śāstra: commentary on a sūtra; treatise on Buddhist philosophy.

śīla: precepts, moral observances, virtuous behavior.

śrāvaka: "hearer," a disciple of the Buddha who understands the basic teachings and follows the path of individual liberation.

śūnyatā: lack of permanent self-existing nature in all things. All things are relative and depend on sets of external causes and conditions for their existence. Often translated as "voidness," or "emptiness."

sūtra: Buddhist scripture, text that contains the actual teachings of the Buddha.

Tathāgata: "one who has come from suchness," one of the epithets of a Buddha.

tathāgatagarbha: "embryo of the Tathāgata," mind's inherent enlightenment that represents the potential of every living being to become a Buddha; suchness manifest in the phenomenal realm.

ten stages: the stages of the Bodhisattva Path which according to the *Avataṃsaka Sūtra* are: joy, freedom from defilement, effulgence, blazing wisdom, hard to conquer, appearance, proceeding far, unmovable, virtuous wisdom, cloud of Dharma.

three realms: the realm of desire, the realm of form, and the formless realm. Also known as the "three worlds."

three times: past, present, and future.

three treasures: the Buddha, the Dharma, and the Saṅgha.

tripiṭaka: the Buddhist canon in which all scriptures are arranged into three divisions: sūtras, Vinaya, and *śāstra*s. Sometimes Abhidharma is taken as the third division of the canon.

two vehicles: see *vehicle.*

vehicle: simile for the Buddha's teaching that carries all living beings to enlightenment and liberation. The two vehicles are the vehicles of the *śrāvaka*s and *pratyekabuddha*s (self-enlightened ones). The three vehicles are these two plus the vehicle of the Bodhisattvas. These three are said to be expedient soteriological contrivances; it is only the One (Buddha) Vehicle that completely discloses the ultimate reality.

Bibliography

Classical Works

An Fa-hsien, trans. *Fo shuo lo-mo-ch'ieh ching*, T 294, vol. 10.

Buddhabhadra, trans. *Ta-fang-kuang fo hua-yen ching.* T 278, vol. 9.

Ch'eng-kuan. *Hua-yen ching shu.* T 1739, vol. 36.

———. *Hua-yen ching shu ch'ao.* Taipei: Hua-yen lien-shih, in 10 vol.

———. *Hua-yen ching sui-shu yen-i ch'ao.* T 1736, vol. 36.

———. *Hua-yen fa-chieh hsüan ching.* T 1883, vol. 45.

Chih-ch'ien, trans. *P'u-sa pen-yeh ching.* T 281, vol. 10.

Chih-yen. *Hua-yen ching sou-hsüan chi.* T 1732, vol. 35.

———. *Hua-yen i-sheng shih hsüan men.* T 1868, vol. 45.

Dharmaraka, trans. *Ju-lai hsing-hsien ching.* T 291, vol. 10.

Fa-tsang. *Hsiu hua-yen ching ao-chih wang-chin huan yüan kuan,* T 1876, vol. 45.

———. *Hua-yen ching chuan-chi.* T 2073, vol. 51.

———. *Hua-yen ching t'an-hsüan chi.* T 1733, vol. 35.

———. *Hua-yen ching wen-i kang-mu.* T 1734, vol. 35.

———. *Hua-yen kuan-mo i-chi,* T 1879, vol. 45.

———. *Hua-yen wu-chio chang.* (Also known as *Hua-yen i-sheng chiao-i fen-ch'i chang.*) T 1866, vol. 45.

———. *Ta-sheng ch'i-hsin lun i-chi.* T 1846, vol. 44.

Feer, M. Leon, ed. *Saṃyutta-Nikāya.* vol. 3. London: Pali Text Society, 1890.

Hui-chiao. *Kao-seng chuan,* T 2059, vol. 50.

Hui-yüan. *Hsü hua-yen ching lueh-shu k'an-ting chi.* HTC vol. 5.

Li T'ung-hsüan. *Hsin hua-yen ching lun.* T 1739, vol. 36.

Lokaskin, trans. *Fo shuo t'u-sha ching.* T 280, vol. 10.

Paramārtha, trans. *Ta-sheng ch'i-hsin lun.* T 1667, vol. 32.

Prājña, trans. *Ta-fang-kuang fo hua-yen ching.* T 293, vol. 10.

Śikṣānanda, trans. *Ta-fang-kuang fo hua-yen ching.* T 279, vol. 10.

Tao-hsüan. *Hsü kao-seng chuan.* T 2060, vol. 50.

Tao-yüan. *Ching-te ch'uan-teng lu.* T 2076, vol. 51.

Tsan-ning. *Sung kao-seng chuan.* T 2061, vol. 50.

Tsung-mi. *Ch'an-yüan chu-ch'üan-chi tou-hsü,* T 2015, vol. 48.

———. *Hua-yen ching hsing yüan p'in shu ch'ao.* HTC vol. 7.

———. *Yüan-chueh ching ta-shu ch'ao.* HTC vol. 14.

———. *Yüan-jen lun.* T 1886, vol. 45.

MODERN WORKS

Broughton, Jeffrey. "K'uei-feng Tsung-mi: Convergence of Ch'an and the Teaching." Ph.D. diss., Columbia University, 1975.

Buswell, Robert E., ed. *Chinese Buddhist Apocrypha.* Honolulu: University of Hawaii Press, 1990.

———, trans. *The Korean Approach to Zen: The Collected Works of Chinul.* Honolulu: University of Hawaii Press, 1983.

Chang, Garma C.C. *The Buddhist Teaching of Totality: The Philosophy of Hwa Yen Buddhism.* University Park: Pennsylvania State University Press, 1971.

Chang Man-t'ao, ed. *Hua-yen ssu-hsiang lun-chi.* Taipei: Ta-sheng wen-hua ch'u-pan she, 1978.

———, ed. *Hua-yen-tsung chih p'an-chiao chi ch'i fa-chan.* Taipei: Ta-sheng wen-hua ch'u-pan she, 1978.

———, ed. *Hua-yen-hsüeh kai-lun.* Taipei: Ta-sheng wen-huach'u-pan she, 1978.

Cleary, Thomas, trans. *The Flower Ornament Scripture.* 3 vols. Boston & London: Shambhala, 1984–1987.

———, trans. *Timeless Spring: A Soto Zen Anthology.* Tokyo: John Weatherhill, Inc., 1980.

———. *Entry Into the Inconceivable: An Introduction to Hua-yen Buddhism.* Honolulu; University of Hawaii Press, 1983.

Cook, Francis H. "Fa-tsang's Treatise on the Five Doctrines—An Annotated Translation." Ph.D. diss. University of Wisconsin, 1970.

———. *Hua-yen Buddhism: The Jewel Net of Indra.* University Park and London: The Pennsylvania State University Press, 1977.

Gimello, Robert M. "Chih-yen (602–668) and the Foundation of Hua-yen Buddhism." Ph.D. diss., Columbia University, 1976.

Gimello, Robert M., and Peter Gregory, eds. *Studies in Ch'an and Hua Yen.* Studies in East Asian Buddhism, no. 1. Honolulu: University of Hawaii Press, 1983.

Gregory, Peter N. *Tsung-mi and the Sinification of Buddhism.* Princeton: Princeton University Press, 1991.

———, ed. *Sudden and Gradual: Approaches to Enlightenment in Chinese Thought.* Honolulu: University of Hawaii Press, 1987.

Hakeda, Yoshito S., trans. *The Awakening of Faith.* New York: Columbia University Press, 1967.

Kamekawa, Kyōshin. *Hua-yen hsüeh.* Chinese trans. by Shih Yin-hai. Hsin-chu, Taiwan: Wu-liang-shou ch'u-pan she, 1988.

———, Liu, Ming-Wood. "The Teaching of Fa-tsang: An Examination of Buddhist Metaphysics." Ph.D. diss., University of California, Los Angeles, 1979.

Kang, Nam Oh. "A Study of Chinese Hua-yen Buddhism with Special Reference to the Dharmadhātu Doctrine." Ph.D. diss. McMaster University, 1976.

King, Sallie B. *Buddha Nature.* Albany: State University of New York Press, 1991.

Ñāṇamoli, Bhikkhu. *The Life of the Buddha.* Kandy, Sri Lanka: Buddhist Publication Society, 1978.

———, trans. *The Path of Purification.* Colombo: R. Semage, 1956.

Prince, A. J. "The Hua-yen Vision of Enlightenment." *Journal of the Oriental Society of Australia,* vol. 15–16 (1983–84), pp. 137–160.

Woodward, F. L. *The Book of Gradual Sayings.* 5 vols. London: Pāli Text Society, 1932–1936.

Yang, Cheng-ho. *Hua-yen-ching chiao yu che-hsüeh yen-chiu.* Taipei: Hui-chu ch'u-pan she, 1980.

Yin Shun, *Ju-lai-tsang-chih yen-chiu.* Taipei: Cheng-wen ch'u-pan she, 1983.

Wisdom Publications

Wisdom Publications is a non-profit publisher of books on Buddhism, Tibet, and related East-West themes. Our titles are published in appreciation of Buddhism as a living philosophy and with the special commitment to preserve and transmit important works from all the major Buddhist traditions.

If you would like more information or a copy of our extensive mail order catalogue, and to keep informed about future publications, please write to us at: 361 Newbury Street, Boston, Massachusetts, 02115, USA.

Wisdom is a non-profit, charitable 501(c)(3) organization and a part of the Foundation for the Preservation of the Mahayana Tradition (FPMT).

Care of Dharma Books

Dharma books contain the teachings of the Buddha; they have the power to protect against lower rebirth and to point the way to liberation. Therefore, they should be treated with respect—kept off the floor and places where people sit or walk—and not stepped over. They should be covered or protected for transporting and kept in a high, clean place separate from more "mundane" materials. Other objects should not be placed on top of Dharma books and materials. Licking the fingers to turn pages is considered bad form (and negative karma). If it is necessary to dispose of Dharma materials, they should be burned rather than thrown in the trash. When burning Dharma, first recite OM, AH, HUNG. Then, visualize the letters of the texts (to be burned) absorbing into the AH, and that absorbing into you. After that, you can burn the texts.

These considerations may also be kept in mind for Dharma artwork, as well as the written teachings and artwork of other religions.